THROUGH CENTRAL BORNEO

TWO YOUNG PENIHINGS, CAUGHT UNAWARES BY MY CAMERA. SUNGEI LOBANG

THROUGH CENTRAL BORNEO

AN ACCOUNT OF TWO YEARS' TRAVEL IN THE
LAND OF THE HEAD-HUNTERS
BETWEEN THE YEARS 1913 AND 1917

BY

CARL LUMHOLTZ

MEMBER OF THE SOCIETY OF SCIENCES OF CHRISTIANIA, NORWAY
GOLD MEDALLIST OF THE NORWEGIAN GEOGRAPHICAL SOCIETY
ASSOCIÉ ÉTRANGER DE LA SOCIÉTÉ DE L'ANTHROPOLOGIE DE PARIS, ETC.

WITH ILLUSTRATIONS
FROM PHOTOGRAPHS BY THE AUTHOR
AND WITH MAP

VOLUME II

NEW YORK
CHARLES SCRIBNER'S SONS
1920

CONTENTS

VOLUME II

CHAPTER XXIII

CONTENTS

CHAPTER XXIX

CONTENTS

ILLUSTRATIONS

ix

THROUGH CENTRAL BORNEO

CHAPTER XXIII

A PROFITABLE STAY—MAGNIFICENT FRUITS OF BORNEO—
OMEN BIRDS—THE PENIHINGS IN DAILY LIFE—TOP
PLAYING—RELIGIOUS IDEAS—CURING DISEASE

On my return to camp a pleasant surprise awaited me
in the arrival of mail, the first in six months. The days
that followed were laborious: buying, arranging, and
cataloguing collections. From early morning Penihings
came to my tent, desiring to sell something, and did not
quit until late at night. Some were content to stand qui-
etly looking at the stranger for ten or fifteen minutes, and
then to go away, their places being taken by others. But
after all it was a happy time, much being accomplished
every day by adding to my collections and gaining much
interesting information.

Over my tent grew a couple of rambutan trees, and
close by were two trees bearing a still more delicate fruit
called lansat (*lansium domesticum*). It is mildly acid,
like the best kind of orange, but with more flavour, and
in appearance resembles a small plum without a stone,
and when ripe is almost white in colour. Every morning,
at my request, the chief climbed one of these trees, on
which the fruit hung by the bushel, and sold me a basket-
ful for a trifle. The lansat is so easily digested that one
can eat it freely in the evening without inconvenience;
in fact it is a decided aid to digestion. According to the
natives these trees are plentiful in the utan, but in the
kampong they, as well as the famous durian and the

rambutan, have been raised from seed. Borneo certainly possesses fine wild fruits, but as the jungle is laborious to pass through it would be most difficult to find the trees. I have hitherto directed attention to the superior quality attained by the fruits of the island which are grown from imported stock, as the pineapple, pomelo, etc.

The usual nuisance of crowing cocks is not to be avoided in a Dayak kampong, though here they were few. I saw a hen running with a small chicken in her beak, which she had killed in order to eat it—a common occurrence according to the Penihings. The ludicrous self-sufficiency of the Bornean male fowls, at times very amusing, compensates to some extent for the noise they make, but they are as reckless as the knights-errant of old. Outside my tent at dawn one morning I noticed one of them paying devoted attention to a hen which was hovering her chickens. He stood several seconds with his head bent down toward hers, then walked round her, making demonstrations of interest, and again assumed his former position, she meanwhile clucking protectingly to her brood. Finally, he resolutely attacked her, where- upon she emitted a discordant shriek while seven or eight tiny yellow chicks streamed forth from underneath her; in response to her cry of distress another cock immediately appeared upon the scene and valiantly chased the dis- turber away.

No less than nine prahus started out one day, bound for Long Iram to buy salt and other goods, taking a small quantity of rattan. The following day, late in the after- noon, the party returned, having passed the night a short distance away. As they had approached Long Blu an omen bird, evidently a small woodpecker, had flown across their path in front of the first prahu, whereupon the whole flotilla at once retraced their course—a tedious day's trip against the current. It makes no difference whether this bird flies from left to right, or from right to left, or whether it crosses in front or behind the boat. If the bird is heard from the direction on the left of the party the augury is bad, whether he is seen or not. If heard from the right side everything is well. After waiting three days the party proceeded on their way.

There are seven omen birds, according to the Penihings, and they are regarded as messengers sent by a good antoh to warn of danger. For the same purpose he may make a serpent pass in front of the prahu, or a rusa cry in the middle of the day. At night this cry is immaterial. The most inauspicious of all omens is the appearance of a centipede. If a man in a ladang is confronted with such an animal he at once stops work there and takes up a new field.

The tribal name of the Penihings is A-o-haeng. Until recently each kampong had from two to five súpi, chiefs or rajas, one being superior to the others. The office was hereditary. There are still several rajas in one kampong, for instance, three in Long Tjehan. The Penihings have a practical turn of mind and though they usually tell the truth at times they may steal. They are the best workers among the tribes on the Mahakam River (above the great rapids) and on a journey they travel in their prahus day and night, resting only a couple of hours in the early morning. However, the custom of travelling at night may be due to fear of meeting omen birds.

The hair of the Penihings and the Oma-Sulings, though it looks black, in reality is brown with a slight reddish tint plainly visible when sunlight falls through it. I believe the same is the case with other Dayak tribes. In Long Tjehan I observed two natives who, though passing as Penihings, were of decidedly different type, being much darker in colour and of powerful build, one having curly hair while that of the other was straight. Penihing women have unpleasantly shrill voices, a characteristic less pronounced with the men. Members of this tribe are not so fine-looking as those of other tribes on the Mahakam, with the exception of the Saputans.

When leaving the kampong on his daily trips to the ladang, or when he travels, the Penihing carries his shield. Even when pig-hunting, if intending to stay out overnight, he takes this armour, leaving it however at his camping-place. A spear is also carried, especially on trips to the ladang. The sumpitan, called sawput, is no longer made and the tribe is not very apt at its use; therefore, being unable to kill the great hornbill themselves, these natives have to buy its highly valued tail feathers from the Punans. The latter and the Bukats, who are the greater experts in the use of the sumpitan, notwithstanding their limited facilities, are also the better makers, which is by no means a small accomplishment. These nomads, and to some extent the Saputans as well, furnish this weapon to all the Bahau tribes, the Kayans excepted.

When meeting, no salutations are made. The mother

uses for her babe the same cradle in which she herself was carried on her mother's back. It is of the usual Dayak pattern, and when it becomes worn or broken a new one is provided, but the old one remains hanging in the house. A cradle is never parted with, because of the belief that the child's life would thereby be imperilled. Should the little one die, the cradle is thrown into the river. An unmarried man must not eat rusa nor fowls, and a married man is prohibited from doing so until his wife has had three children. Men should not touch with their hands the loom, nor the ribbon which is passed round the back of the woman when she weaves, nor should a woman's skirt be touched by a man. These precautions are taken to avoid bad luck in fishing and hunting, because the eyesight is believed to be adversely affected by such contact. Their sacred number is four.

An unusual game played with large tops is much practised for the purpose of taking omens in the season when the jungle is cleared in order to make new ladangs. The top (bae-ang) is very heavy and is thrown by a thin rope. One man sets his spinning by drawing the rope backward in the usual way; to do this is called niong. Another wishing to try his luck, by the aid of the heavy cord hurls his top at the one that is spinning, as we would throw a stone. To do this is called maw-pak, and hence the game gets its name, maw-pak bae-ang. If the second player hits the spinning top it is a good omen for cutting down the trees. If he fails, another tries his luck, and so on. The long-continued spinning of a top is also a favourable sign for the man who spins it. With the

Katingans a hit means that it is advisable to cut the trees at once, while a miss necessitates a delay of three days. Every day, weather permitting, as soon as the men return from the ladangs in the evening, about an hour before sunset, this game is played on the space before the houses of the kampong. Sometimes only two men consult fate, spinning alternately. The same kind of top is found among the Kayans, Kenyahs, and other Dayak tribes.

According to the information I obtained from the Dayaks they believe that the soul has eternal existence, and although many tribes have the idea that during life several souls reside in one individual, after death only one is recognised, which is generally called liao. One or more souls may temporarily leave the body, thereby causing illness.

Neither in this life nor the next are there virtuous or sinful souls, the only distinction being in regard to social standing and earthly possessions, and those who were well-to-do here are equally so there. With the Katingans whatever is essential to life in this world is also found in the next, as houses, men, women, children, dogs, pigs, fowls, water-buffaloes, and birds. People are stronger there than here and cannot die. The principal clothing of the liao is the tatu marks, which it will always keep. The garments worn besides are new and of good quality. When my informant, a native official of Kasungan, who sports semi-civilised dress, expressed his disapproval of the poor wearing quality of his trousers to an old Katingan, the latter exclaimed: "That matters not. Above, all new ones!" In the belief of the Duhoi (Ot-Danums) the liao remains with the body until the funeral-house falls into decay, perhaps for twenty years, when it enters the soil and "is then poor." The idea of the Penihings about life after death is vague, and they do not pretend to know where the soul goes.

The Penihings acknowledge five souls, or batu, in each individual: one above each eye, one at either side of the chest below the arm, and one at the solar plexus. The souls above the eyes are able to leave their abiding-place, but the others can go only short distances. If the first-named depart the person becomes ill next day, the immediate cause being that a malevolent antoh, desiring to eat the victim, has entered the head through the top. On perceiving this the two souls located above the eyes escape and the blian is called upon to bring them back, for unless they return the afflicted one will die.

A fowl or a pig, or both, may then be killed and the blood collected. Some of it is smeared on the patient's forehead, head, and chest, the remainder being offered to antoh, both in plain form and mixed with uncooked rice, as has been described on page 202. When a fowl is sacrificed the empty skin, suspended from a bamboo stalk, is likewise reserved for antoh, the meat having been consumed, as usual, by those concerned.

As another effective means of inducing the return of the soul the blian sings for several hours during one night or more. In the Penihing tribe he accompanies himself by beating an especially made stringed shield. It is be-

lieved that the singer is able to see how the antoh caused
the sickness: whether he did it by throwing a spear, by
striking with a stick, or by using a sumpitan.   In his
efforts to restore the patient the blian is told what to sing
by a good antoh that enters his head.   Without such
help no person can sing properly, and the object of the
song is to prevail upon a beneficent spirit to eject or kill
the evil one so that the souls may return.

The blian usually resorts also to feats of juggling, proceeding in the following way: Clasping his open hands
forcibly together over the painful part, at the same time
turning himself round and stamping on the floor, he
wrings his hands for a few seconds and then, in sight of
all, produces an object which in the Penihing conception
represents a bad antoh—in fact, by them is called antoh.
In this manner he may produce several bits of substance
which are thrown away to disappear.   According to
belief, when the blian performs his trick it is in reality
a good antoh that does it for him.

While we were in camp at Long Tjehan there was considerable singing at night for the cure of sick people, and
four voices could be heard in different parts of the house
at the same time.   One night I was prevented from sleeping by a remedial performance just above my tent, which
was only a few metres from the house.   The clear, strong
voice of the blian had resounded for an hour or more,
when five loud thumps upon the floor were heard, as if
something heavy had fallen.   The fact was that the man
had stamped hard with his right foot as by sleight-of-
hand he caught various objects from the patient, produc-

ing in quick succession a piece of wood, a small stone, a fragment of bone, a bit of iron, and a scrap of tin. Five antohs, according to the Penihing interpretation, had been eradicated and had fled. Afterward he extracted some smaller ones in a similar manner but without stamping his foot. The singing was then continued by another man and a woman, in order to call the friendly antoh, that the exercises might be happily concluded.

The blian also tries to placate the malevolent antoh by the gift of food. A Penihing informant said that the evil one also eats the sacrificial blood, including that which is smeared on the patient, and ultimately may leave satisfied. As soon as the souls see that the antoh has gone they return and the victim recovers. The blian's remuneration is usually one parang and a handful of rice. If the person is very ill, a gong and a handful of rice is the fee, but should the patient die the gong is returned. The Duhoi (Ot-Danum) women occasionally put on men's costume, and vice versa, to frighten the antoh that causes illness and keep it at a distance. With the Katingans a good antoh is believed to reside in the saliva applied by the blian for healing purposes to that part of a body which is in pain. The saliva drives out the malevolent antoh, or, in other words, cures the pain.

CHAPTER XXIV

HEAD-HUNTING, ITS PRACTICE AND PURPOSE

THE Penihings still live in dread of the head-hunting raids of the Ibans of Sarawak, and the probability of such attacks no doubt caused the recent establishment of a garrison at Long Kai. The Long-Glats on the Merasi, a northern tributary to the Mahakam, are also constantly on guard against the Ibans. Until lately these inveterate head-hunters would cross the mountains, make prahus, then travel down the Upper Mahakam, and commit serious depredations among the kampongs, killing whomsoever they could, the others fleeing to the mountains. As one Penihing chief expressed it to me: "The river was full of their prahus from the Kasao River to Long Blu." Their last visit was in 1912, when the Bukats reported that a number of Ibans had arrived at the headwaters of the river, but the raid did not materialise, and they retired without making prahus. These raids have naturally brought about much intermingling of the tribes on the Mahakam River, and sometimes three or more may be found living in one kampong.

About twenty years ago there was much fighting in these remote parts of Borneo among Penihings, Saputans, Penjabongs, and Bukats, each tribe making head-hunting raids into the dominions of another, and all being constantly exposed to the fury of the Ibans from the north.

Head-hunting raids may include assaults on kampongs, but very often they are cowardly attacks on small groups of unsuspecting people, men, women, and children. The heads thus secured appear to be as highly valued as those acquired under more heroic conditions. The fact is also noteworthy that the heads of Malays are appreciated, but, with few exceptions, not those of white people. Several times I heard of Malay rattan or rubber gatherers who had been disposed of in that way. The head is severed by one stroke.

As a typical case of head-hunting I give the following description of a raid which, twelve years previous to my visit, was made by ten Bukats upon a small party of Saputans who were on a babi hunt. Among the Penyahbongs, Saputans, Punans, and Penihings a woman may accompany her husband or another man on the chase, carry a spear, and assist in killing pig or deer. Bear she does not tackle, but, as my informant said, "even all men do not like to do that." She also carries her own parang, with which she may kill small pigs and cut down obstacles in her path. The hunting-party, one man and three women, had been successful. The babi had been killed with spears and, in accordance with custom, the head had been cut off with a parang. The carcass had been cut up and the three women carried the meat in the coarse-meshed rattan bags on their backs, while the man bore the head on his shoulder, all homeward bound, when the Bukats attacked them. Only one woman escaped.

The slayers hurried off with the three heads, being afraid of the people of the kampong which was not far away. As usual the heads were tied by the hair to the handle of the shield, and were thus carried to the place where the rattan bags had been left, inside of which they were then placed.

After taking heads the men are on the run for two or three days, travelling at night with torches, and in the evening they make a big fire to dry the heads. The brains, because of the weight, may have been taken out the first evening; this is done through the foramen, and a hole is made with a spear point in the top of the skull. The hair has first been cut off and taken care of, to be tied as ornaments to shields or plaited round the handle of the sword. The Katingans, however, throw away the hair with the flesh. Apprehensive of pursuit, they may dry the head but a little while each night, grass being tied round it when carried. Sometimes damar is used to dry the flesh and the eyes.

The last night out the head-hunters always sleep near their kampong, and early next morning, while it is still dark, they come singing. The people of the kampong waken, array themselves in their best finery, and go to meet them, the women wearing their newest skirts and bringing pieces of nice cloth to present to the conquerors. The man who cut the head carries it suspended from his neck until it is taken from him by a woman who gives him the cloth to wear instead, possibly as a badge of heroism. It makes no difference whether this service is performed by his wife, an unmarried woman, or another man's wife. The singing ceases and all proceed to the kampong, to the house of the kapala, where the heads are hung from the beam at the head of the ladder, and the cloths which were bestowed upon the victors are returned to the women.   The heads are left hanging, while for the festivities connected with their arrival a hut, called man-gosang, is constructed, consisting of an airy shelter made of two rows of bamboo stalks supported against each other, and profusely adorned with the inevitable wood shav-ings.

The head-hunters, who must take their food apart from their associates and in the presence of the heads, now bring water from the river to boil rice, in bamboo, outside on the gallery.   When the cooking is finished the heads are brought to take part in the meal, being hung near the place where the men are to eat and about half a metre above the floor, to be out of reach of dogs.   A pinch of rice is put into the hole at the top of the skull and the head is addressed in the following words: "Eat this rice first.   Don't be angry.   Take care of me.   Make this body of mine well."   During the period of restrictions imposed on the hunters the heads remain at the same place, sharing the meals as described.

For twelve days the hunters do no work and refrain from eating meat, vegetables, fish, salt, and red pepper, rice being the only permissible food.   They are obliged to take their food on the gallery, and those who have never been on such expeditions before must also sleep there during that time.   A man who has taken part three or more times may join his wife, but he must take his meals on the gallery.   When twelve days have passed no more food is given to the heads, which are hung on the beam again, three to five being placed together in a rattan basket, with leaves around them. At the triennial festival, tása, blood of pig or fowl mixed with uncooked rice, is offered to the heads.

Usually the head-hunting raids were, and are still to a limited extent, carried far away into distant regions and may occupy several months. The Saputans, who were devotees to the custom, would go as far as the river Melawi in the southwest to Sarawak in the north, as well as to the Murung or Upper Barito River in the east. Sometimes only two to five men would go, but usually there were about ten—an equal number remaining behind in the kampong. Controleur W. J. Michielsen, quoted before, relates an instance of a Dayak from Serayan, whose daughter had been killed by a Katingan head-hunter, who pursued the marauders to their homes, and, on the occasion of the festivities incident to the return of the members of the raid, he cut the head from the murderer of his child while the celebration was in progress. His action was so sudden that they were totally unprepared, and no attempt was made to prevent his escape with the head.

In times gone by when a Saputan man, woman, or child died it was the custom for a member of the family to go forth to look for a head. In the case of an ordinary person one was deemed sufficient, but for a chief five to ten were necessary. When taking a head a cut was made in the slain man's chest with a parang; into the wound the raiders then put their forefingers and sucked the blood from them.

Each head-hunter carried rice in a rattan basket, but he depended for food mainly on sago-palms and wild animals that were killed. After such an expedition has been determined upon, the preparations may occupy a year or even longer, but usually about three months. When all is ready for a start, a delay of from one to four days may be caused by unfavourable interference of an omen bird. Should a bird chance to repeat the omen when another start is made, the party must return to the kampong and wait a long time. The Dayaks are very much guided in their actions by omens taken not only from birds but also from incidents, and merely to hear a certain bird is sufficient reason to change all plans.

When leaving their kampong to take part in an expedition to New Guinea the Penihings heard the cry of a bird called tarratjan, and requested the lieutenant in charge to wait four days. He replied, naturally, that the Company (government) does not employ birds in making decisions, and while the Dayaks offered no further objection they declared to him that one of them would surely die. According to my informant it so happened that before arriving at the island one man died. If at such a time a large tree should be seen falling, he said, then they would like to give up the trip to New Guinea entirely, but being afraid of the Company they go, notwithstanding the warning.

If a head-hunting party sees a large tree fall, the expedition is abandoned, and no young men who took part can ever join another venture of the same kind. Old and experienced men, after the lapse of a year, may resume operations. In case of meeting a centipede a head-hunting expedition must return immediately to the kampong, and for four years no such enterprise may be undertaken.

The purposes of head-hunting are manifold. The slain man is believed to change into a servant and assistant in the next life. When a chief dies it becomes an essential duty to provide him with heads, which are deposited on his grave as sacrifices, and the souls of which serve him in the next life. Heads taken for the benefit of kampong people are hung in the house of the kapala to counteract misfortune and to confer all manner of benefits. An important point is that the presence of the heads from other tribes, or rather of the souls residing in them, compels evil antohs to depart. A kampong thus becomes purified, free from disease. The killing of a fowl is not sufficient to accomplish this; that of a pig helps a little, a water-buffalo more, but to kill a man and bring the head makes the kampong completely clean.

With the Katingans a head hanging in the house is considered a far better guardian than the wooden figures called kapatongs, which play an important part in the life of that tribe. Any fear of resentment on the part of the liao (departed soul) residing in the head is precluded by their belief that the Katingan antoh gave him the order to watch.

"If no heads are brought in there will be much illness, poor harvest, little fruit, fish will not come up the river as far as our kampong, and the dogs will not care to pursue pigs," I was told by a Penihing who had taken part in a head-hunt and served his sentence in Soerabaia. "But are not people angry at losing their heads?" I asked him. "No," he answered, "we give the heads food on their arrival and every month afterward, and make fire every evening to keep them warm. If they feel cold, then they get angry." The man who has taken a head is considered a hero by the women, and if unmarried is certain to secure a desirable wife, but it is erroneous to assert that the taking of a head was or is a necessary condition to marriage.

The government of the Dutch Indies, with energy and success, is eradicating the evil head-hunting custom. Military expeditions involving great expense from time to time are sent into remote regions to capture a handful of culprits. By exercising tact it is not difficult finally to locate the malefactors, and indeed the tribe may deliver them. It must be remembered that the Dayaks themselves have no idea that there is anything wrong in taking heads, and the government very wisely does not impose the death penalty, but the transgressor is taken to Soerabaia, on Java, to undergo some years of hard labour—from four to six, I understand. To " go to Soerabaia" is extremely distasteful to the natives, and has proved a most effective deterrent. On account of their forced stay at this remote island city such Dayaks learn to speak Malay and several times I have employed them. They are usually among the best men of the kampong, resourceful, reliable, and intelligent, and may serve also as interpreters.

In his report on a journey to the Katingans in 1909 Captain J. J. M. Hageman says:

"By nature the Dayak is a good-tempered man. The head-hunting should not be charged against him as a dastardly deed; for him it is an adat. In the second place, he possesses very good traits of character, as evidenced by his hospitality and generosity. Our soldiers, some sixty in number, obtained a meal immediately in every kampong. When a Dayak goes on a journey in a friendly region he may be sure of receiving shelter and food in every house.

"They are distrustful of foreigners, but if he has gained their confidence they give assistance freely in every respect. Loving their liberty in a high degree they prefer not to be ordered. The cowardly manner in which they cut heads is no criterion of their courage."

It would not be in accordance with facts to suppose that head-hunting has altogether been eliminated in Borneo. It is too closely identified with the religious life of the natives, but in time a substitute probably will be found, just as the sacrifice of the water-buffalo supplanted that of slaves. The most recent case that came to my notice on the Mahakam was a Penihing raid from Long Tjehan to the Upper Barito five years previously, in which four Murung heads were taken.

It is extraordinary that such a revolting habit is practised in a race the ethics of which otherwise might serve as a model for many so-called civilised communities, these natives being free to an unusual degree from the fault of appropriating what belongs to others and from

untruthfulness. The fact that the Dayaks are amiable
in disposition and inclined to timidity renders this phase
of their character still more inexplicable. The inevitable conclusion is that they are driven to this outrage
by religious influences and lose their self-control. As of
related interest I here note what Doctor J. M. Elshout,
who had recently returned from Apo Kayan, communi-
cated to me. He had spent three years at the garrison
of Long Nawang among the fine Kenyahs and spoke the
language. "As soon as one enters upon the subject of
taking heads one no longer knows the Kenyah. Of his
mild and pacific disposition little or nothing remains.
Unbounded ferocity and wantonness, treachery and
faithlessness, play a very great part; of courage, as we
understand the meaning of the word, there is seldom a
trace. It is a victory over the brua (soul) of the man
who lost his head, and the slayer's own brua becomes
stronger thereby. If opportunity is given they will take
heads even if they are on a commercial trip. Outsiders,
even if they have been staying a long time in the kampong, run a risk of losing their heads."

CHAPTER XXV

DEPARTURE FROM THE PENIHINGS—FRUIT-EATING FISH—
ANOTHER CALL AT LONG PAHANGEI—A TRIP UP THE
MERASI RIVER—GENIAL NATIVES—AN INOPPORTUNE
VISIT—THE DURIAN, QUEEN OF ALL FRUITS

IT became expedient to prepare for our farther journey
down the river, but first I wanted to take some photographs and measurements of the kampong people; this,
however, proved an impossible task because of the adverse influence of the reticent and conservative Raja
Paron, who spoke not one word of Malay. Recently he
had been shocked by the sale to me of two live specimens
of the curious spectacled lemur (*tarsius borneanus*), which
had been added to my collections. The raja was incensed with the man who sold them, because the makiki,
as these animals are called, are regarded as antohs, and
in their anger at being sold were making people ill.
Therefore these new proceedings for which his sanction
was asked were regarded by him with disapproval, and as
a result of his opposition the people began to disappear
in the direction of their ladangs. Fortunately, I had
secured good material in both respects from Long Kai,
and I began preparations for departure.

Prahus and a sufficient number of men were secured,
and in the middle of July we started. On the Mahakam
there never was any difficulty about getting men who
were eager to gain their one rupia a day. The difficulty

was rather the other way, and this morning the prahus were found to contain more paddlers than had been agreed upon, and seven surplus men had to be put ashore. On the river-banks at this time were noticeable trees bearing small fruit of a yellowish-red colour, and which were so numerous as to impart their hue to the whole tree. Violent movements in the branches as we passed drew our attention to monkeys, which had been gorging themselves with fruit and scampered away on our approach. Birds, naturally, like the fruit, and, strange to say, it is a great favourite with fish, many kinds of which, chiefly large ones such as the djelavat and salap, gather underneath the trees in the season. On the Mahakam and the Katingan this is an occasion for the Dayaks to catch much fish with casting-net, spears, or hooks. The tree, which in Malay is called crevaia, is not cut, and there is no other known to the natives the fruit of which the fish like to eat. Though not sweet, it is also appreciated by the Dayaks.

Another singular observation made on the Mahakam was the effect of dry weather on the jungle. At one place, where it covered hills rising from the river, the jungle, including many big trees, looked dead. From what I later learned about the burning of the peat in Sarawak, where unusually dry weather may start fires which burn for months, this was undoubtedly also the case here, but it seems strange that in a country so humid as Borneo the weather, although admittedly of little stability, may become dry enough to destroy the woods in this manner.

I had decided to pay another short visit to Long

Pahangei, where we arrived in the afternoon, and again we were among Oma-Sulings. Some good specimens were added to my ethnographic collections, among them wearing apparel for both sexes said to be over a hundred years old and which I bought from the Raja Besar, who was visiting here. He possessed a number of old implements and weapons of considerable interest. The raja of a near-by kampong arrived on his way to Long Iram, and the largest of his seven prahus was of unusual dimensions, measuring, at its greatest width, 1.34 metres over all. Although the board, four centimetres thick, stands out a little more than the extreme width of the dugout, which is the main part of a prahu, still the tree which furnished the material must have been of very respectable size.

The Raja Besar showed great desire to accompany me on an excursion up the Merasi River, a northern affluent within the domain of the same tribe. My preference was for Lidju, my constant assistant, but on the morning of our start the great man actually forced himself into service, while the former, who had been told to come, was not to be seen. The raja began giving orders about the prahus and behaved as if he were at home. As I remained passive he finally said that he wanted to know whether he could go; if I preferred Lidju he would remain behind. Not wanting a scene, and as he was so intent on going, I gave the desired permission. Though, like the others, he was nude except for a loin-cloth, Raja Besar was a gentleman at heart, but he did not know how to work, especially in a prahu. On account of his exalted position he had never been accustomed to manual labour, but always to command. He naturally selected a place in my prahu and seated himself at one side, which kept the boat tilted; however, it was out of the question for any of the men to correct him. When the prahu moved away the first thing he did was to wash his feet, next his hands and arms, finally to rinse his mouth, and several times during the trip the performance was repeated. He was of little assistance except through the authority that he exerted as a great raja.

Early in the afternoon we arrived at Lulo Pakko (lulo = river; pakko = edible fern), situated in a beautiful hilly country. The natives very obligingly helped to make camp in the usual way. Raja Besar, who made himself at home in the gallery of the long communal house, told me that he wanted his "children," as he called the men, to remain until the following day, his plan being to obtain double wages for them. With the swift current, however, they could easily return the same day, so I said I had no objection to their staying, but that they would receive no extra pay for the additional time; whereupon they left without argument.

Comfortably established on the cool, spacious gallery of the large house, I received articles they were willing to sell, had decorative designs interpreted for me, and interviewed the more intelligent of these pleasant Oma-Sulings. On the floor lay an admirably finished plank, which was used as a seat; it was about four centimetres thick and nearly two metres broad, the bark remaining on the edges. In Long Pahangei I noticed a similar one of slightly narrower width.

The women, who were genial in their manners, came to my tent constantly to ask for tobacco, which evidently was a great luxury with them, and sometimes they were even troublesome. One afternoon when all was ready for my bath, which I always take at one side of the tent opening, three young women came and seated themselves just outside. While the natives are always welcome and I like them, yet I was not prepared, after a hard day's work, to relinquish my bath in order to receive a visit from even attractive ones of the fair sex. There was simply nothing to do but to disregard their presence. Calmly I began to take off my clothes, as if the ladies were not there. At first my preparations seemed to make no impression whatever, but finally, when I was about to divest myself of the last of my few garments, they smiled and went away.

This was the season for the durian fruit and we much enjoyed this delicacy, of which Mr. A. R. Wallace, fifty years ago, wrote: "To eat durians is a new sensation, worth a voyage to the East to experience." There were some superb trees seventy metres high growing not far from my tent, and many others farther away. The people of the Mahakam do not climb these tall trees to get the fruit, but gather them from the ground after it has fallen. One night I heard one fall with a considerable crash. Roughly speaking, it is of the size of a cocoanut; a large one might kill a man and has been known to cause serious injury. It is most dangerous for children to walk under the trees in the fruit season.

The durian is intensely appreciated by the natives,

THE DURIAN TREE, WITH FRUIT. LULO PAKKO, ON THE MERASI RIVER

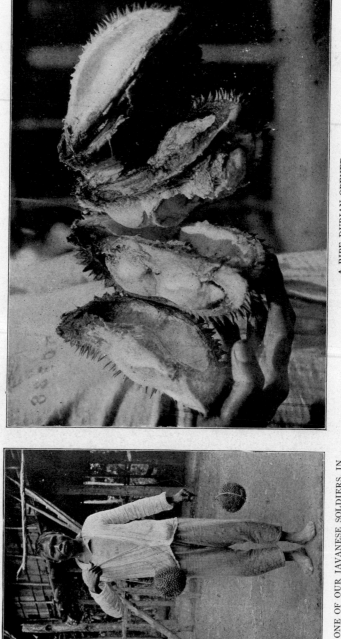

A RIPE DURIAN OPENED

ONE OF OUR JAVANESE SOLDIERS, IN UNDRESS, CARRYING TWO DURIANS. LULO PAKKO, MERASI RIVER

and tatu marks representing the fruit are strikingly prominent in Central Borneo. It also has its European devotees, though most of them take a dislike to it on account of its strong odour, resembling that of decayed onions. On my arrival in Batavia one of my first trips had been to the market to buy a durian, which I brought to the hotel with anticipation of great enjoyment. My disappointment was great, its taste being to me as offensive as its odour. Nobody knows what a durian is like until he eats one that has been permitted to ripen and fall to the ground. Even in Java this would be difficult, unless one made special arrangements with the natives who bring them to the market-places. It is popularly supposed that the durian is an aphrodisiac, but that is not the case. Any food or fruit that one greatly enjoys acts favourably on the digestive organs, and therefore makes one feel in vigorous condition.

Those that were brought to me on this occasion, and which had just fallen from the tree, were of a fresh green colour with a streak of yellow here and there and had a pleasant, rich odour. The most satisfactory way to eat it is with a spoon; the pulp, though rich, is not heavy, and, moreover, is stimulating. It serves the purpose of a dessert, with a flavour and delicacy that is indescribable and that makes one feel happy. Among the great enjoyments of life are the various delicious fruits when really ripe and of the best grade, but comparatively few people have that experience. The vast majority are perfectly satisfied to eat fruit that was picked green and matured afterward. Many years ago I tasted a real orange from New-South-Wales, and ever since I have disdained the more acid kind.

My firmness in refusing to pay the men for more time than was necessary produced a salutary effect upon Raja Besar. He fixed fair prices on things I wanted to buy, which before he had not done, and I made him tie labels on the specimens I bought. As he was truthful, he finally served as well as Lidju. On the last day of our stay he helped me to repress the eagerness of the Dayaks to "turn an honest penny." The prahus, besides being defective, were not large enough for many men, and I was determined not to have more than three in each, a quite sufficient number when going downstream. I have a suspicion that he objected to four for reasons of personal safety.

Owing to the rapid current, we made the return voyage in two hours, and when we got to the Mahakam River we found it very much swollen, with logs floating downstream beside us. Our low-lying prahus were leaking and the situation was not agreeable, though I should have felt more anxious had I not been with Dayaks, who are extremely able boatmen. At Long Pahangei the captain from Long Iram, who is also the controleur of that district, had arrived and was waiting on account of the overflow of the river. I had an hour's talk with this pleasant man, who thinks that the Dayaks on the Upper Mahakam ultimately must die out because they do not have enough children to perpetuate the tribe. He said that in 1909, when he was stationed at Puruk Tjahu, nothing was known about the country where we then were.

The Oma-Sulings, according to their traditions, came from Apo Kayan nearly two hundred years ago. Oma means place of abode; Suling is the name of a small river in Apo Kayan. They had at the time of my visit six kampongs on the Upper Mahakam, the largest of which is Long Pahangei, with about 500 inhabitants. Material for clothing is no longer woven, but is bought in Long Iram. This is probably also the case with the Long-Glats, but the Penihings still do some weaving.

CHAPTER XXVI

AMONG THE LONG-GLATS—IS FEAR OF EXPOSURE TO THE
SUN JUSTIFIED?—CHARACTERISTICS OF THE LONG-
GLATS—GOOD-BYE TO THE MAHAKAM

IN the latter part of July we went to the near-by kampong, Long Tujo ("a small animal with many legs"),
situated at the mouth of another small tributary to the
Mahakam. Here live Long-Glats who are located below
the other Bahau peoples of the river and are found as
far as Batokelau, between the upper and lower rapids.
Though Long Iram is rather distant—five days' travel
down-stream, and, if the river is high, perhaps two months
may be consumed in returning—still its influence was
evidenced by the several umbrellas I saw, all black, an
adaptation from the high-class Malays and an unusual
sight in these parts. The kapala of this large kampong
resembled a Malay raja, in that he always carried an
umbrella when he walked and looked pale because the
sun was not allowed to shine upon him. Two days later,
when I photographed the ladies performing dances, they
had at least five of these fashionable contrivances.

It may be stated that natives of the Dutch Indies
are generally afraid of the sun. Well-to-do Malays carry
umbrellas as a protection against it. In Batavia I read
in the newspapers that the Sultan of Priok, when visiting
an aviation camp, was so overcome by the heat that he
had to be carried away, regaining consciousness on arriv-

ing at his quarters. However, the attack may have been induced to some extent by general lack of exercise and the indolent life that characterises his compatriots who occupy high positions.

Even some of the pagan tribes protect their heads, as the Katingans, the Duhoi, and others, who make beautiful sunshades, which also serve in case of rain, and this was not learned from the Malays. In the Bornean tribes that I visited, until the child is old enough to walk, the sun is not allowed to shine upon it even for a moment. The blacks of Australia, on the other hand, who are in a state of absolute nudeness, pay no attention to the sun, though in common with most natives of hot countries they usually prefer to follow the example of the animals and remain quiet in the middle of the day.

An umbrella of the usual type, Chinese or Japanese, is very useful for travel in Borneo. At times it proves of excellent service in the prahu in case of sudden showers, and it is invaluable for protecting the camera when photographing. But as a matter of comfort and convenience it is my custom to have my head uncovered except in rainy or cold weather. The sun is a great friend and health-giver, and notwithstanding well-meant warnings and an inborn fear first to be overcome, during my journeys in Borneo I carried my hat in my pocket. When travelling in a prahu, I do not care for a prolonged exposure to the sun, but often I photographed for three or four hours continuously—really hard work—in the blazing light of the equatorial sun, without experiencing any disagreeable effect. In the spring of 1910 I

travelled in this way for three months, mostly on horse-
back, through the Sonora Desert, and felt stronger for it.
It is my opinion that overfatigue, excess in eating, or
alcohol are the causes of sunstroke. I have met only
one man who, like myself, discards cover for the head—
Doctor N. Annandale, of the Indian Museum in Calcutta.
Although in our present state of knowledge I agree with
him that it is unwise to advise others to do likewise in
the tropics, I emphatically recommend less fear of the
sun in temperate regions, always on the supposition that
one leads a healthy and sane life.

The Long-Glats came from Apo Kayan, and established themselves first on the River Glit, a tributary from
the south to the River Ugga, which again is an affluent
to the River Boh, the outlet from Apo Kayan to the
Mahakam. Since that time the people have called themselves Long-Glit, which is their correct name, but as they
have already become known as Long-Glat, through the
Dutch, I shall use that designation.

In the kapala's house I saw a superb plank, four
metres long, raised lengthwise against the wall; one side
of it was taken up with fine carvings on a large scale,
representing three pairs of dogs. This I fortunately
obtained. The kapala's father was an Oma-Suling, but
his grandmother, a Long-Glat, had taught him some
kremi or kesa, the Malay words for folklore (in Long-
Glat, lawong), and I collected from him two rather interesting tales, which are included with other folklore stories
at the end of this book. In one of them (No. 18) the
airplane is foreshadowed, and by one that could fly for a

THREE LONG-GLAT WOMEN OF THE NOBILITY. LONG TUJO

Side View

The tail feathers of the rhinoceros hornbill are usually emblems of warriors and blians

Front View

The ornaments around the hips and on the sash and hem of the skirts are silver coins

LONG-GLAT WOMEN. LONG TUJO. FRONT VIEW

Notice the earrings purchased from the Malay traders, especially in the left-hand figure

BACK VIEW OF THE LONG-GLAT WOMEN

The hair ornament hanging over the back of the central figure is notable and was not found in any other tribe on the journey

month, at that.   Needless to state, an airplane had never
been heard of in those parts.

The people were inquisitive but more distant than the
other tribes I had visited, a quality which is often a sav-
ing grace.   They were very willing to be photographed,
and among my subjects were three women of the nobility,
called rajas, who had many coins sewn on their skirts in
a way that looked quite well.   One wore a head ornament such as I had not seen before, an elaborate affair
lying over the hair, which was worn loose and hanging
down the back.   One man trembled noticeably when before the camera, without spoiling the photograph, however, though it was a side-view.

Of the women who helped me with the interpretations
of designs, one had a marked Mongolian fold of the eye,
though her eyes could scarcely be said to be placed obliquely.   As far as my observations go, the Mongolian
fold is very slight with the natives of Borneo, or not
present at all, and the obliquity of the eyes is seldom
striking.   The Long-Glats do not tatu much, many not at
all, but generally they have on the left upper arm a picture of the nagah in its usual representation with the
disproportionately large dog's mouth.   Wild cattle are
not eaten here.   The great hornbill, as well as the red
and white hawk, may be killed, but are not eaten.

Three times a day the women bring water and take
baths, while the men bathe when fancy dictates.   Penihing and Kayan women begin to husk rice about five
o'clock in the morning, while it is still dark.   That is
pemáli (forbidden) among the Long-Glats, but the women

cook rice at that hour, and, after eating, most of
the people depart to the ladangs, returning about four
o'clock in the afternoon.   The women who remain in the
kampong place paddi on mats in the sun to dry, and at
noon they husk rice.   Early in the afternoon, and again
about two hours after sunset, meals are served, consisting
always of boiled rice and a simple stew of boiled vegetables of one or more kinds (called sayur, a Malay word),
and sometimes pork.

In the evening the women may cut rattan into fine
strips, or weave these into mats, while the men employ
themselves in making a sheath for a parang, or an axe-
handle, or carving a hilt for a sword, etc.   They talk
till late at night and sometimes sing.   None of the Bahau
people are able to make rattan mats of such exquisite
finish as the Long-Glats.   The beautiful dull-red colour
employed is procured from a certain grass which is crushed
and boiled, the rattan being kept in the infusion one day.
The black colour is obtained by the same method from the
leaves of a tree, and both colours are lasting.

In the belief of the Long-Glats, people should not
laugh at animals, lest some misfortune result.   For instance, when dogs fight among themselves or with cats,
one should not indulge in mirth, else the thunder, which
is an antoh, becomes angry and makes somebody ill.
In this kampong was a young hornbill which was quite
domesticated and frequently came to rest on the top of
my tent.   It often fought the hens and even the dogs,
which was an amusing sight, but would carry disquieting
significance to the Dayak who allowed himself to laugh.
The lieutenant from Long Kai possessed a very tame

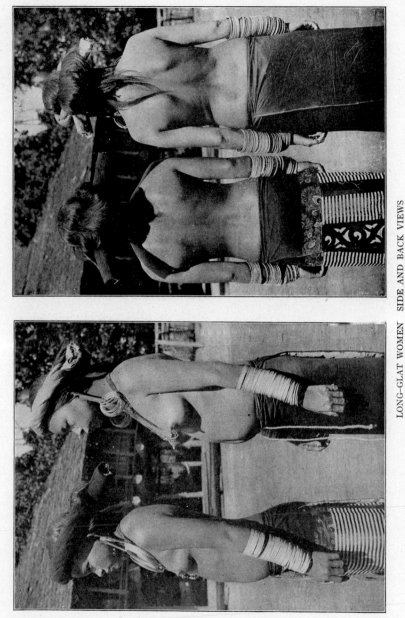

LONG-GLAT WOMEN   SIDE AND BACK VIEWS

The heavy ornaments for the ears, consisting of rings hung from the vastly distended lobes, are much beloved by the Dayak women.   Those of the men are usually smaller and fewer in number

LONG–GLATS, WITH A NATIVE DOG. LONG TUJO

wah-wah which had accompanied him on a visit here. The natives told me that a child had become ill because she could not help laughing at the ape when it ran after the lieutenant and climbed one of his legs. According to the blian, the little girl was very warm and feverish, but he sang in the night, and next day she was well.

Considerable similarity is evident in customs, manners, and beliefs of the Long-Glats and the Oma-Sulings, though the limited time at my disposal did not permit me fully to investigate this subject. Bear-meat is not eaten by either, and rusa (deer) and kidyang are not killed, the latter especially being avoided. Sumpitans are bought, and blians' shields such as the Penihings have are not made. Both these tribes pray for many children, which to them means larger ladangs and much food. The wish of these peoples is to have ten children each. In view of the fact that in Long Pahangei the number of women was disproportionately small, the desire for large families seemed unlikely to be gratified. Many men, some of them old, were unmarried, but no women were single. Twins sometimes occur, but not triplets. The mother nourishes her offspring for about five years, the two youngest suckling at the same time. A raja may marry ten women, or more, and has a great marriage-feast of more than a week's duration. Lidju, my Long-Glat assistant, said that his father had fifteen wives, his grandfather thirty, but it was no longer the fashion to have so many. The common man (orang kampong) is allowed only one wife. Divorces are easily obtained, and neither suicide nor abortion is known.

July is supposed to be the dry season, but rarely a day

passed without showers. One evening occurred the heaviest thunder-storm I experienced in Borneo. It came from the west and was accompanied by a great downpour, straining my tent to the utmost. The sergeant one day brought in a large lizard (*varanus*) which he shot from the prahu just as it was about to enter the river. Its length was 2.30 metres; the circumference back of the fore legs 44 centimetres.

It was with regret that I said good-bye to the Bahau peoples. Had it been in my power, I should like to have spent years instead of months in this Mahakam region. The Dayaks here are friendly to strangers, and as the great rapids farther down the river form a natural barrier, they seldom receive visitors, therefore are little changed by outside influence. The Malays have never been able to extend their influence above the rapids, and whatever modification may be noticeable in the natives is chiefly due to their journeys to Long Iram in order to exchange the products of the utan for commodities of the outside world. The government has exerted itself to keep the Malays from coming, but no doubt in the end this will prove as unavailing as it did on the Upper Barito. A few of them now and then find their way across the range that forms a natural boundary toward the south, and although thus far Malay settlement up here is negligible, its ultimate ascendancy is probable, however long the time that may pass before it is accomplished.

CHAPTER XXVII

CONTINUING THE JOURNEY DOWN THE RIVER—GREAT
KIHAMS—BATOKELAU—AT LONG IRAM—LAST STAGES
OF OUR JOURNEY—ARRIVAL AT SAMARINDA—HINDU
ANTIQUITIES—NATIVE'S SUPERIORITY TO CIVILISED
MAN

EARLY in August, as soon as the river had receded
sufficiently to be considered favourable for travel, we
started in seven prahus with thirty-two men. After
less than two hours' swift journey we encountered the
advance-guard of the kihams, which, though of little
account, obliged us to take ashore almost all our goods,
and we walked about fifteen minutes. It seemed a very
familiar proceeding. Early in the afternoon we arrived
at the kubo, a desirable shelter that had been erected
at the head of the first great kiham, but its limited accom-
modations were taxed to overflowing by our arrival.
Already camped here were a few Buginese traders and a
raja from the Merasi River, accompanied by two good-
looking wives, who were all going to Long Iram and had
been waiting two days for the river to fall. The raja, who
presented me with some bananas, moved with his family
a little farther down the river, and I put up my tent as
usual.

Next morning the transportation of our goods on
human backs was begun, and shortly after six o'clock I
started with the men to walk to the foot of the rapids,
which takes about three hours. On the way, I observed

277

a large accumulation of vines and branches heaped round the base of a tall trunk which at first sight looked dead. The tree to all appearances had died, all the branches had fallen, and with them the vines, orchids, ferns, etc., that had lived on it, but after being rid of all this burden it came to life again, for at the top appeared small branches with large leaves. A singular impression was created by the big heap of vegetable matter, not unlike a burial-mound, from the midst of which emerged the tall, straight trunk with the fresh leaves at the top, telling the tale of a drama enacted in the plant world through which the tree had passed triumphantly.

My camping-place was a small clearing on the high river-bank, where I remained two days while the goods were being transported. There had been little rain for a few days; indeed, it is possible the dry season had begun, and the weather was intensely hot, especially in the middle of the day. I catalogued a number of photographic plates, but the heat in my tent, notwithstanding the fly, made perspiration flow so freely that it was difficult to avoid damage. Moreover, I was greatly annoyed by the small yellow bees, which were very numerous. They clung to my face and hair in a maddening manner, refusing to be driven away. If caught with the fingers, they sting painfully.

The river fell more than one metre during the first night, and the Merasi raja's party passed in their prahus at seven o'clock next morning. At twelve our seven prahus showed up, bringing some large packages that could easiest be spared in case anything happened. The following day the remainder of the baggage arrived, carried on the backs of the men, and I was glad to have all here safe and dry.

In a couple of hours we arrived in the kampong Batokelau (turtle), and below are other rapids which, though long, are less of an obstacle. A beautiful mountain ridge, about 1,200 metres high, through which the river takes its course, appears toward the southeast. The population includes fifty "doors" of Busangs, forty "doors" of Malays, and twenty of Long-Glats. Crocodiles are known to exist here, but do not pass the rapids above. The kapala owned a herd of forty water-buffaloes, which forage for themselves but are given salt when they come to the kampong. When driven to Long Iram, they fetch eighty florins each. The gables of the kapala's house were provided with the usual ornaments representing nagah, but without the dog's mouth. He would willingly have told me tales of folklore, but assured me he did not know any, and pronounced Malay indistinctly, his mouth being constantly full of sirin (betel), so I found it useless to take down a vocabulary from him.

Continuing our journey, we successfully engineered a rapid where a Buginese trader two weeks previously had lost his life while trying to pass in a prahu which was upset. Afterward we had a swift and beautiful passage in a canyon through the mountain ridge between almost perpendicular sides, where long rows of sago-palms were the main feature, small cascades on either side adding to the picturesqueness. At the foot of the rapids we made camp in order to enable me to visit a small salt-water accumulation in the jungle a couple of kilometres farther down the river. As we landed near the place, we saw over a hundred pigeons leaving. There were two kinds of these birds at the pool, most of them of a very common large variety, with white head and green wings, and all were shy; according to the opinion of the Dayaks, owing to the prevalence of rain.

Next morning we started shortly after six o'clock, and early in the afternoon reached the kampong Omamahak, which is inhabited by Busangs, with a sprinkling of Malays. Two hours later twenty-one prahus arrived from Apo Kayan with one hundred and seventy-nine Kenyahs on their way to Long Iram to carry provisions to the garrison. Soon afterward the captain of Long Iram overtook us here, returning from his tour of inspection above, so the place became very populous. The next night we stopped at Hoang Tshirao, inhabited by a tribe of the same name, also called Busang, apparently quite primitive people. The kampong was neat and clean; there were many new wooden kapatongs, as well as small wooden cages on poles, evidently serving for sacrificial offerings. The following day we arrived at Long Iram.

Of comparatively recent origin, the town lies on level land, and its inhabitants outside the garrison are Malays, Chinese, and Dayaks. The street is long, extremely well kept, and everything looks orderly and clean, while before the captain's house were many beautiful flowers. The pasang-grahan, which is in a very quiet locality, is at-

tractive and has two rooms. One was occupied by an
Austrian doctor in the Dutch military service, who was
on his way to Long Nawang, while I appropriated the
other. He was enthusiastic over the superb muscles of
the Kenyahs who had just arrived and were camping in
a house built for such occasions on top of a small hill a
short distance away. Cows, brown in colour, were graz-
ing in a large field near by, and I enjoyed the unusual
luxury of fresh milk—five small bottles a day. After I
had bathed and put on clean garments, even though my
linen-mesh underclothing was full of holes, I felt content
in the peaceful atmosphere.

The doctor of Long Iram, who had been here one
year, told me that no case of primary malaria had come
to his notice. What the Malays call demum is not the
genuine malaria, but probably due to the merotu, a
troublesome little black fly. One of his predecessors had
collected 1,000 mosquitoes, out of which number only 60
were anopheles. There was framboisia here, for which
the natives use their own remedies. The temperature at
the warmest time of the day is from 90° to 95° Fahren-
heit; at night, 75° to 80°. There is much humidity, but
we agreed that the climate of Borneo, especially in the
interior, is agreeable.

It was extraordinary how everything I had brought
on this expedition was just finished. The day before I
had had my last tin of provisions; the milk was gone except ten tins, which would carry me through to Samarinda,
a four days' journey; the candles were all used; the supply of jam exhausted; tooth-brushes no longer service-

able; my clothes in rags.   Fortunately I had more stores in Bandjermasin.   The rot-proof tents which I bought in England were to some extent a disappointment because they deteriorated even though not in actual use, or possibly because of that fact.   On account of the delay caused by the war the bulk of my considerable tent outfit was not unpacked until two years after purchase.   It had been carefully kept, but was found to be more or less like paper, and only a small portion could be used.   One tent served me throughout Bornean travels, but finally the quality of the fabric became impaired to a degree which necessitated constant patching; it was made to last only by the exercise of great care and with the aid of a fly, three of these having been used on this expedition.   If a journey to a country climatically like Borneo is planned to last only a year, rot-proof tents may be recommended on account of their light weight and great convenience.

The enterprising Kenyahs offered to sell me the model of a raja's funeral-house which seven of them made while there.   Most of the material evidently had been brought with them.   It was an interesting sample of their handicraft.   At the house of the first lieutenant I was shown several similar models, some with unusual painted designs, which were eloquent testimonials to the great artistic gifts of this tribe.   I also bought a small earthen jar.   One of the natives who was able to speak some Malay said that such ware is common in Apo Kayan and is used for cooking rice.   The poison for the dart of the blow-pipe is also boiled in earthenware vessels.   The jars, which are sometimes twenty-five centimetres in diameter, are protected on journeys by being encased in rattan netting. The Kenyahs are perhaps the most capable of all the natives of Borneo. Of the one hundred and seventy-nine visiting members of the tribe, only one was afflicted with the skin diseases so prevalent among many of the other Dayaks, and, according to Doctor J. M. Elshout, syphilis is not found among those of Apo Kayan.

The steamship connection with Samarinda is irregular, and as a small transport steamer was making ready to take away its usual cargo of rattan and rubber, I decided to avail myself of the opportunity. The commercial products are loaded in a fair-sized boat, which is made fast to the side of the steamer, and a similar one may be attached to the other side. Such boats, which are called tonkang, also take passengers, mostly Malay and Chinese, but there are no cabins, and the travellers spread their mats on the limited deck according to mutual agreement.

A swarm of Kenyahs began at seven o'clock to convey our baggage, and the soldiers later reported that there was not even standing-room left. I climbed on board and found rattan piled high everywhere, covering even the steps that led up to the "passenger-deck," where I emerged crawling on all fours. A shelter of duck had been raised for me in one corner, the lieutenant and Mr. Loing placed their beds in the adjoining space, while the soldiers camped next to them. All the natives, packed closely together, formed another row.

The most necessary of my belongings were stored inside the shelter, and there I passed the four days quite comfortably. On account of many noises, including that made by the engine, reading was impossible, so I employed the time in mending two suits of my precious linen-mesh underwear which was rapidly going to shreds, without prospect of opportunity to replace them in the Far East. Morning and afternoon the Malays on deck held their Mohammedan services, apparently singing in Arabic, and during the night the sailors sang much. There were two rough bath-rooms, but I bathed only once, as I was afraid of losing my slippers or other articles that were liable to drop into the river through the intervals between the narrow boards of the floor.

We travelled steadily day and night, but stopped at many kampongs to take on more cargo, and an additional tonkang was attached, which relieved some of the congestion on ours. One afternoon the monotony was relieved by a fight in the kitchen of the little steamer, when a sudden thumping sound of nude feet against the floor was heard and boiled rice flew about. But it was very soon over, evidently only an outburst of dissatisfaction with the cook; somebody called for the Malay captain and we heard no more about it.

There was a Bombay Mohammedan merchant on board who had small stores of groceries and dry-goods on the Kutei River, as the Mahakam is called in its lower course. He also spoke of the hundreds of thousands of Hindus who live in South Africa. On the last day of our journey a remarkably tame young snake bird was brought on board, which one of the sailors bought. According to reports, there are many of these birds on the river. He tied it to the stern railing until night, when he put it on top of the cargo, apprehending that it might try to dive if tempted by the constant sight of the water. When asleep it curled itself up in an extraordinary manner, the long neck at first glance giving it a serpent-like appearance. It cried for fish and showed absolutely no fear.

On August 22, 1916, we arrived at Samarinda. The custom-house authorities permitted me to put our numerous packages in the "bom." The lieutenant and Mr. Loing went to a new Chinese hotel, while I, in a prahu, paddled to the pasang-grahan, a spacious building with several rooms. Our journey through Central Borneo had been successfully concluded, and during nine months we had covered by river 1,650 kilometres, 750 of these in native boats.

During my absence the great war had become more real to the Archipelago through the occasional appearance in Bornean waters of British and Japanese cruisers. I heard of a German who walked from Bandjermasin to Samarinda because he was afraid of being captured if he went by steamer. The journey took him six weeks. It was my intention, while waiting here a few days for the steamer, to visit a locality farther down the river which is marked on the map as having Hindu antiquities. The kapala of the district, who had been there, was sent for, and as he said that he had neither seen nor heard of any such relics, which probably would have to be searched for, I relinquished the trip. Hindu remains, which locally were known to be present in a cave north of Samarinda, had been visited in 1915 by the former assistant resident, Mr. A. W. Spaan, whose report on the journey was placed at my disposal. The cave is in a mountain which bears the name Kong Beng, Mountain of Images, due probably to a local Dayak language. It lies in an uninhabited region four days' march west of Karangan, or nearly two days' east of the River Telen, the nearest Dayaks, who are said to be Bahau, living on the last-named river. During the time of Sultan Suleiman six or seven statues were taken from Kong Beng to Batavia and presented to the museum there.

The country traversed from the River Pantun, to follow Mr. Spaan's account, at first is somewhat hilly, changes gradually into undulating country, and finally into a plain in the middle of which, quite singularly, rises this lonely limestone mountain, full of holes and caves, about 1,000 metres long, 400 broad, and 100 high, with perpendicular walls. The caves are finely formed and have dome-shaped roofs, but few stalactite formations appear. Thousands of bats live there and the ground is covered with a thick layer of guano. From the viewpoint of natural beauty these caves are far inferior to the well-known cave of Kimanis in the Birang (on the River Berau, below the Kayan) with its extraordinarily beautiful stalactite formations. In one of the caves with a low roof were found eleven Hindu images; only the previous day the regent of Kutei had turned the soil over and recovered a couple more archæological remains. Ten of these relics are in bas-relief and about a metre high. The eleventh, which is lower, represents the sacred ox and is sculptured in its entirety. One bas-relief from which

A NARROW-SNOUTED CROCODILE SHOT BY OUR SERGEANT BELOW THE GREAT RAPIDS OF THE MAHAKAM

ENTRANCE TO THE CAVE OF KONG BENG

At work in the self-filling basins

Washing for the precious stones

MAYLAYS SEARCHING FOR DIAMONDS AT MARTAPURA

From kinematograph films

the head had been broken struck the observer as being finely executed; he recognized four Buddhas, one Durga, and one Ganesha.

Another cave visited was noteworthy on account of a strong wind which continually issues from it and for which he was unable to account. The current is formed in the opening, and twenty-five metres back of it there is no movement of the atmosphere. The cave is low, but after ten minutes' walk it becomes higher and has connection with the outside air. There it is very high, and the sun's rays falling in produced a magnificent effect, but no wind was noticeable there. Standing in front of this cave a strange impression was created by the sight of leaves, branches, and plants in violent movement, while outside there was absolutely no wind.

I should much have liked to visit Kong Beng, but circumstances prevented my doing so, though the assistant resident, Mr. G. Oostenbroek, courteously offered his small steamer to take me up along the coast. Some months later an American friend, Mr. A. M. Erskine, at my instigation made the journey, and according to him it would take a month to properly explore the locality. The man whom the Sultan of Kutei sent with him threw rice on the statues, and the accompanying Dayaks showed fear of them. By digging to a depth of about a metre and a half through the layer of guano, a pavement of hewn stone was found which rested on the floor of the cave. That the trip proved interesting is evident from the following description submitted to me:

"The weird experience of those two nights and one day in the huge caves of Kong Beng can never be forgotten. The caves were so high that my lanterns failed to reveal the roof. There were hordes of bats, some of them with wings that spread four feet. The noise of their countless wings, upon our intrusion, was like the roar of surf. Spiders of sinister aspect that have never seen the light of day, and formidable in size, were observed, and centipedes eight or nine inches long. In places we waded through damp bat guano up to our knees, the strong fumes of ammonia from which were quite overpowering.

"Far back in one of the caverns were those marvellous Hindu idols, beautifully carved in bas-relief on panels of stone, each with a projection at the bottom for mounting on a supporting pedestal. They represent the Hindu pantheon, and are classic in style and excellent in execution. They are arranged in a half-circle, and high above is an opening to the sky which allows a long, slanting shaft of light to strike upon their faces. The perfect silence, the clear-cut shaft of light—a beam a hundred feet long—drifting down at an angle through the intense darkness upon this group of mysterious and half-forgotten idols, stamps a lasting picture upon one's memory.

"It is the most majestic and strangely beautiful sight I have ever seen. Coming upon the noble group of gods gazing at the light, after a long dark walk through the cave, gives one a shock of conflicting emotions quite indescribable. One hardly dares to breathe for fear of dispelling this marvellous waking dream. Fear and awe, admiration and a sense of supreme happiness at having a wild fancy turn to reality, all come over one at once. A single glance at this scene was ample reward for all the long days and nights of effort put forth to reach it. I never again expect to make a pilgrimage of this sort, for only one such experience can be had in a lifetime."

It is rather surprising that Hindu remains in Borneo should be found at such an out-of-the-way place, but Doctor Nieuwenhuis found stone carvings from the same period on a tributary to the Mahakam. Remains of Hindu red-brick buildings embedded in the mud were reported to me as existing at Margasari, southwest of Negara. Similar remains are said to be at Tapen Bini in the Kotawaringin district.

In 1917, at the Dayak kampong Temang, in the district of that name, Mr. C. Moerman, government geologist, saw a brass statue fifteen centimetres high, which appeared to him to be of Hindu origin. Before being shown to visitors it is washed with lemon (djeruk) juice. When on exhibition it is placed on top of rice which is contained in a brass dish more than twenty-five centimetres in diameter. After being exhibited it is again cleaned with lemon-juice and then immersed in water which afterward is used as an eye remedy. One must give some silver coin for the statue to "eat." Its name is Demong (a Javanese word for chief) Akar. Originally there were seven such Demongs in that country, but six have disappeared.

Hindu influence is evident among the Dayaks in the survival of such names as Dewa and Sangiang for certain good spirits. In the belief of the Katingans, the departed soul is guarded by a benevolent spirit, Dewa, and it is reported from certain tribes that female blians are called by the same name. A party of Malays caught a snake by the neck in a cleft of a stick, carried it away and set it free on land instead of killing it, but whether this and similar acts are reminiscent of Hindu teaching remains to be proven.

At the end of August we arrived in Bandjermasin, where several days were spent in packing my collections. For many months I had been in touch with nature and natural people, and on my return to civilisation I could not avoid reflective comparisons. Both men and women of the Mahakam have superb physiques; many of them are like Greek statues and they move with wonderful, inborn grace. When with them one becomes perfectly familiar with nudity and there is no demoralising effect. Paradoxical as it may sound, the assertion is nevertheless true, that nothing is as chaste as nudity. Unconscious of evil, the women dispose their skirts in such fashion that their splendid upper bodies are entirely uncovered. Composed of one piece of cloth, the garment, which reaches a little below the knee and closes in the back, passes just over the hips, is, as civilised people would say, daringly low. It is said that the most beautiful muscles of the human body are those of the waist, and among these natives one may observe what beauty there is in the abdomen of a well-formed young person.

It is an undeniable fact that white men and women compare unfavourably with native races as regards healthful appearance, dignity, and grace of bearing. We see otherwise admirable young persons who walk with drooping shoulders and awkward movements. Coming back to civilisation with fresh impressions of the people of nature, not a few of the so-called superior race appear as caricatures, in elaborate and complicated clothing, with scant attention to poise and graceful carriage. One does not expect ladies and gentlemen to appear in public in "the altogether," but humanity will be better off when healthful physical development and education of the intellect receive equal attention, thus enabling man to appear at his best.

CHAPTER XXVIII

AN EARTHQUAKE—ERADICATING THE PLAGUE—THROUGH
THE COUNTRY NORTHEAST OF BANDJERMASIN—MARTA-
PURA AND ITS DIAMOND-FIELDS—PENGARON—THE
GIANT PIG—THE BUKITS—WELL-PRESERVED DECORA-
TIVE DESIGNS—AN ATTRACTIVE FAMILY

I DECIDED to travel more in Borneo, but before undertaking this it was necessary for several reasons to go to
Java. In Soerabaia I had my first experience of an
earthquake. Shortly before two o'clock, while at lunch-
eon in the hotel, a rather strong rocking movement was
felt, and I looked at the ceiling to see if there were cracks
which would make it advisable to leave the room. But
it lasted only a few seconds, although the chandeliers
continued to swing for a long time. At other places
clocks stopped, and I read in the papers that the vibra-
tion passed from south to north, damaging native vil-
lages. In one town the tremors lasted three minutes and
were the worst that had occurred in thirty-four years,
but when the disturbance reached Soerabaia it was far
less severe than one experienced in Los Angeles, Cali-
fornia, in April, 1918.

As is well known, the government of the Dutch Indies
expends millions in eradicating the plague, which is prevalent in portions of eastern Java. In addition to exter-
minating the rats, it is necessary to demolish the bamboo
huts of the natives and move the inhabitants to new

quarters. Houses of wood are erected, lumber for the purpose being imported from Borneo in great quantities. That the efforts have been crowned with success is indicated from the reports issued in 1916, showing that plague cases had been reduced seventy per cent.

Returning to Bandjermasin toward the end of October, I began to make arrangements for a journey to Lok Besar, in a hilly region of the Northeast at the source of the Riam Kiwa River. This kampong had recently been visited by the government's mining engineer, Mr. W. Krol, on one of his exploring expeditions. At first glance it might seem unpromising to make researches in a region so near to a stronghold of the Malays, but as he was the first and only European who had been in the upper country of that river, there was a fair chance that the natives might prove of considerable interest. It was a matter of five or six days by prahu from Bandjermasin, followed by a three days' march, and I decided to return by a different route, cross the mountain range, and emerge by Kandangan.

Accompanied by Mr. Loing, the surveyor, and the soldier-collector, I started from Bandjermasin on November 1. To travel by the canal to Martapura can hardly be regarded as a pleasure-trip, as mosquitoes and flies are troublesome. Half a year later I went by the road to the same place under more cheerful conditions, and though the day was overcast, the flooded country just north of the town presented a picturesque appearance. Rows of high-gabled Malay houses, with narrow bridges leading out to them, were reflected in the calm water, and beautiful blue morning-glories covered the small bushes growing in the water. Along the road were forests of *melalevca leucodendron*, of the family of *myrtaceæ*, from which the famous cajuput-oil is obtained. It is a very useful, highly aromatic, and volatile product, chiefly manufactured in the Moluccas, and especially appreciated by the Malays, who employ it internally and externally for all ailments. They are as fond of cajuput-oil as cats are of valeriana.

Early in the afternoon the prahus landed us at Marta-pura, which is renowned for its diamonds and once was the seat of a powerful sultanate. The fields, which have been known for a long time, cover a large area, and the diamonds found in gravel, though mostly small and yellow, include some which are pronounced to be the finest known to the trade. There is always water beneath the surface, and natives in bands of twenty occupy themselves in searching for the precious stones, digging holes that serve besides as self-filling basins in which the gravel is panned. The government does not work the fields. In a factory owned by Arabs the diamonds are cut by primitive but evidently very efficient methods, since South African diamonds are sent here for treatment, because the work can be done much cheaper than in Amsterdam.

The controleur, Mr. J. C. Vergouwen, said that there were 700 Dayaks in his district. He was able to further my plans materially by calling a Malay official who was about to start in the same direction for the purpose of vaccinating the natives some distance up country. The kapala of the district, from Pengaron, who happened to be there, was also sent for, and both men were instructed to render me assistance. Next day the Malay coolies carried our baggage to the unattractive beach near the market-place, strewn with bones and refuse, loaded our goods in the prahus, and the journey began. The men were cheap and willing but slow, and it was near sunset when we arrived at the English rubber plantation near Bumirata.

The controleur had been friendly enough to send word to the manager that he had invited me to stay overnight at the estate. However, upon arrival there we were told that the manager had gone to Bandjermasin the day before, but was expected back at seven o'clock. It did not seem the proper thing to make ourselves at home in his absence, so we returned to the kampong, five minutes below by prahu, to make camp in a spacious, rather clean-looking, shed that formed the pasar or market-place.

At midnight I was awakened by the halting of an automobile and a Malay calling out, "Tuan! Tuan!" and I stepped from my bed to meet a friendly looking man in a mackintosh, who proved to be Mr. B. Massey, the manager. We talked together for an hour in the calm of a Bornean night. What he said about the irregularity of the climatic conditions interested me. Two years previously it had been so dry for a while that prahus could move only in canals made in the river-bed. His friends had thought him mad to come to Borneo, but he liked the climate better than that of Java. His kind invitation to breakfast I declined with regret, because when one is travelling it is very troublesome to change clothing, shave, and appear civilised.

We arrived at Pengaron at noon. The kapala of the district, a Malay with the title of kiai, lived in a comfortable house formerly occupied by a controleur, one room serving the purpose of a pasang-grahan. On our arrival he was at the mosque, but returned in an hour. The vaccinateur was already there, and by a lucky chance Ismail made his appearance, the kapala from Mandin, whom the controleur thought would be useful, as he had influence with Malays and Dayaks. The kiai, a remarkably genial man, was the most agreeable Malay I met. He behaved like an European, bathed in the bathroom, à la Dutch, dressed very neatly, and had horses and carriage. The hours were told by a bell from four o'clock in the morning, and two clocks could be heard striking, one an hour ahead of the other.

In the afternoon, Mr. Krol, the mining engineer, returned from a trip of a month's duration, wearing a pedometer around his neck. He had walked twenty miles in the jungle that day. A Dayak who had accompanied him from Pa-au, one day's march toward the east, gave me some information about the giant pig, known to exist in Southern Borneo from a single skull which at present is in the Agricultural High School Museum of Berlin. During my Bornean travels I constantly made inquiries in regard to this enormous pig, which is supposed to be as large as a Jersey cow. From information gathered, Pa-au appears to be the most likely place where a hunt for this animal, very desirable from a scientific point of view, might be started with prospect of success. An otherwise reliable old Malay once told me about a pig of extraordinary size which had been killed by the Dayaks many years ago, above Potosibau, in the Western Division. The Dayaks of Pa-au, judging from the one I saw and the information he gave, are Mohammedans, speak Malay, and have no weapons but spears.

The vaccinateur started in advance of us to prepare the people for our arrival. Our new paddlers, who were jolly and diligent men, brought their rice packed in palm-leaves, one parcel for the men of each prahu. They use leaves of the banana even more frequently for such purposes, as also do Javanese and Dayaks, and spread on the ground they form a neat and inviting setting for the food, serving the purpose of a fresh table-cloth. The men ate rapidly with their fingers and afterward drank water from the kali (river), throwing it into the mouth with the hand, as is the Malay custom. I did not notice that they brought dried fish, which is the usual complement to a meal. In this section of the country there is much admixture of blood between Dayaks and Malays, which accounts for the fact that the latter are more genial and agreeable than their lower classes usually are. At Pinang the small population turned out in full force, standing picturesquely near the mosque on an open space between the cocoanut-trees that grew on the high river-bank. It was evident that visitors are not often seen there.

At Belimbing the usually steep, high river-bank had been made accessible by short sticks so placed as to form steps that led up almost perpendicularly. Great was my surprise to find myself facing an attractive little pasang-grahan, lying on grassy, level ground at almost the same height as the tops of the cocoanut and pinang palms on the other side of the river. It was a lovely place and charmingly fresh and green. The house, neatly built of palm-leaves, contained two rooms and a small kitchen, with floors of bamboo. In the outer room was a table covered with a red cloth and a lamp hung above it, for the Malays love the accessories of civilisation. The kapala and the vaccinateur were there to receive us, and we were treated as if we were officials, two men sleeping in the house as guard. I was told there are no diseases here except mild cases of demum (malaria) and an itching disorder of the skin between the fingers.

On the fourth day from Martapura we arrived at the first Dayak habitation, Angkipi, where Bukits have a few small bamboo shanties consisting of one room each, which were the only indications of a kampong. The most prominent feature of the place was a house of worship, the so-called balei, a square bamboo structure, the roomy interior of which had in the centre a rectangular dancing-floor of bamboo sticks. A floor similarly constructed, but raised some twenty-five centimetres higher, covered about all the remaining space, and serves as temporary habitations for the people, many small stalls having been erected for the purpose. Our friend the vaccinateur was already busy inside the building, vaccinating some fifty Dayaks from the neighbouring hills and mountains who had responded to his call. When I entered, they showed

MALAY HOUSE, NEAR MARTAPURA

This type shows the so-called Bandjermasin style of a gabled roof

MALAY HOUSE AT MANDIN

BUKIT WOMEN. MANDIN

Cleansing themselves from the evil effects of being photographed

timidity, but their fears were soon allayed, and I made myself at home on the raised floor, where I had a good camping-place.

Although these Bukits, among whom I travelled thereafter, are able to speak Malay, or Bandjer, the dialect of Bandjermasin, they have preserved more of their primitive characteristics than I expected. As I learned later, at Angkipi especially, and during a couple more days of travel, they were less affected by Malay influence than the Dayaks elsewhere on my route. The kampong exists only in name, not in fact, the people living in the hills in scattered groups of two or three houses. Rice is planted but once a year, and quite recently the cultivation of peanuts, which I had not before observed in Borneo, had been introduced through the Malays. Bukits never remain longer than two years at the same house, usually only half that time, making ladang near by, and the next year they move to a new house and have a new ladang. For their religious feasts they gather in the balei, just as the ancient Mexicans made temporary habitations in and near their temples, and as the Huichols and other Indians of Mexico do to-day.

The natives of Angkipi are stocky, crude people. Several had eyes set obliquely, *à la* Mongol, in a very pronounced manner, with the nose depressed at the base and the point slightly turned upward. Among the individuals measured, two young women were splendid specimens, but there were difficulties in regard to having them photographed, as they were all timid and anxious to go home to their mountains.

Next day, marching through a somewhat hilly country, we arrived at the kampong Mandin on the River Lahanin. Here was the residence of Ismail, to whose influence probably was due the recent conversion to Islam of several families. The pasang-grahan, though small, was clean and there was room for all. Thanks to the efforts of the vaccinateur, the Dayaks, who were very friendly, submitted to the novel experience of the camera and kept me busy the day that we remained there. A great number of women whom I photographed in a group, as soon as I gave the signal that it was all over, rushed with one impulse to the river to cleanse themselves from the evil effects of the operation.

As the Bukits are not very strong in carrying burdens, we needed fifty carriers, and Ismail having assisted in solving the problem, the march was continued through a country very much cut up into gulches and small hills. Time and again we crossed the Riham Kiwa, and went down and up gullies continually. At a small kampong, where I took my midday meal sitting under a banana-tree, the kapala came and in a friendly way presented me with a basket of bananas, for these Dayaks are very hospitable, offering, according to custom, rice and fruit to the stranger. He told me that nearly all the children were ill, also two adults, but nobody had died from a disease which was raging, evidently measles.

At Ado a harvest-festival was in progress in the balei, which, there, was of rectangular shape. Within I found quite elaborate preparations, among which was prominently displayed a wooden image of the great hornbill.

There was also a tall, ornamental stand resembling a candelabrum, made of wood and decorated with a profusion of long, slightly twisted strips of leaves from the sugar-palm, which hung down to the floor. From here nine men returned to our last camping-place, where they had left a similar feast in order to serve me. The harvest-festival is called bluput, which means that the people fulfil their promise to antoh. It lasts from five to seven days, and consists mostly of dancing at night. Neighbouring kampongs are invited and the guests are given boiled rice, and sometimes babi, also young bamboo shoots, which are in great favour and are eaten as a sayur. When the harvest is poor, no feast is made.

The balei was very stuffy, and little light or air could enter, so I continued my journey, arriving later in the afternoon at Beringan, where a tiny, but clean, pasang-grahan awaited us. It consisted mainly of four small bamboo stalls, in which there was room for all of us to sleep, but the confined air produced a disagreeable congestion in my head the next day. We now had to send for men to Lok Besar, which was our ultimate goal, and the following day we arrived there, passing through a country somewhat more hilly than hitherto. I put up my tent under some bananas, and felt comfortable to be by myself again, instead of sleeping in crowded pasang-grahans. There was not even such accommodation here, but the kapala put most of his little house at our disposal, reserving only a small room and the kitchen for himself and family. The boiling-point thermometer showed an elevation of 270 metres.

I had a meeting with the blians, who knew nothing worth mentioning. Almost everything had been forgotten, even the language, still it is remarkable how primitive these people remain, and there is scarcely any mixture of Malay apparent in the type. For two or three days the kind-hearted, simple people gathered in numbers at the middle kampong of the three which bear the same name, Lok Besar, upper, middle, and lower. The Dayaks call the upper one Darat, which means headwaters.

One man had a skin formation which at a superficial glance might be taken for a tail. It was about the size of a man's thumb, felt a little hard inside, and could be moved either way. On the outside of each thigh, over the head of the femur, was a similar but smaller formation. Another man had an excrescence on each thigh, similarly located, but very regular in shape, forming half a globe; I saw a Dayak on the Mahakam with the same phenomenon. One woman had such globular growths, though much smaller, in great numbers on the feet.

Among the Bukits I observed two harelipped men, one hunchback, and an unusual number of persons with goitre. These natives drink water by the aid of a leaf folded into an improvised cup. Eight of the upper front teeth are cut. Suicide is not known. Their only weapon at present is the spear, which they buy very cheaply from the Malays, but formerly the sumpitan was also in use. To hunt pig they have to go some distance into the mountains; therefore, they seldom undertake it. Honey is gathered by climbing the tree in which the bees' nest is discovered.

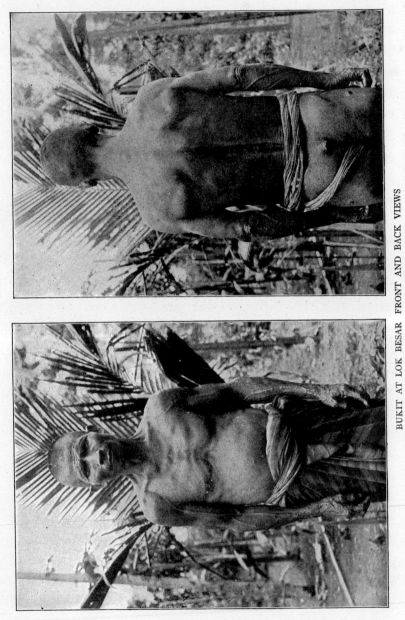

BUKIT AT LOK BESAR FRONT AND BACK VIEWS

Skin formation giving the appearance of a short tail. Globular growths on each thigh are also seen

BUKIT WOMAN AND HER TWO SONS. LOK BESAR

She was one of the very few remaining women able to give correct information in regard to
decorative designs

Bamboo pegs are inserted in the trunk at intervals and a rope made from a certain root is tied between them, thus forming a ladder upon which the natives ascend the tree at night. The women make rattan mats, and also habongs or receptacles in which to carry the mats when travelling.

Fire is extinguished for the night. These natives sleep on a single mat, made from either bamboo or rattan, and usually nothing is placed under the head, but sometimes small wooden blocks are used. In the morning when they arise they roll the mats, and the chamberwork is done. A young girl whom I measured had her hair fastened up with the quill of a porcupine; when asked to undo her hair, she put the quill under the top of her skirt. The Bukits possess one musical instrument, sarunai, a kind of clarinet, which does not sound badly. There are many bliano, nearly all men. Several prominent members of the tribe asserted that head-hunting was never practised—at least there is no tradition concerning it.

A man may have one, two, or three wives. When a young man is poor, he pays two ringits or two sarongs to his bride's father, but half that amount is sufficient for a woman no longer youthful. The usual payment appears to be twelve ringits or twelve sarongs, which the blian at the wedding places on top of his head, while with his right hand he shakes two metal rings provided with rattles. On the Barito I noted the same kind of rattles used on a similar occasion. He asks Dewa not to make them ill, and a hen as well as boiled rice is sacrificed to this antoh. The dead are buried in the ground as deep as the height of a man. Formerly the corpse was placed in a small bamboo house which rested on six upright poles, and on the floor a mat was spread.

I was pleasantly surprised one day when a Dayak arrived at our kampong bringing a number of attractive new bamboo baskets which he had bought on the Tappin River, near by to the west. He was going to finish them off by doing additional work on the rims and then carry them to Kandangan, where they would fetch about one guilder each. All were of the same shape, but had different designs, and he knew the meaning of these— there was no doubt about it—so I bought his entire stock, thirteen in number. I learned that most of the people were able to interpret the basket designs, but the art of basket-making is limited, most of them being made by one or two women on the Tappin. A very good one, large and with a cover, came from the neighbouring lower kampong. An old blian sold it to me, and his wife softly reproved him for so doing, but when I gave her ten cents as a present she seemed very well satisfied.

For the interpretation of these designs I found an excellent teacher in a gentlewoman from the lower kampong. She had extensive knowledge concerning this matter, an impression later confirmed by submission of the baskets to another woman expert from the Tappin, of repute as a maker and for knowledge of the designs. I hope that in due time my informant will receive the photograph of herself and her boys which I shall send to her in grateful recognition of her valuable assistance. Her name was Dongiyak, while her good husband was called

Nginging. She had two attractive and extremely well-behaved sons of twelve and fourteen years, who trusted implicitly in her and showed absolute obedience, while she was kindness itself coupled with intelligence. In fact their relations were ideal, and it seemed a pity that these fine boys should grow to manhood and die in dense ignorance.

I doubt whether any traveller, including the honest missionary, disagrees with the terse sentence of the great Wallace in *The Malay Archipelago*: "We may safely affirm that the better specimens of savages are much superior to the lower examples of civilised peoples." Revolting customs are found, to be sure, among native races, but there are also redeeming virtues. Is there a so-called Christian community of which it may be truly said that its members do not steal, as is the case with the majority of Dayak tribes? There are savage races who are truthful, and the North American Indians never broke a treaty.

In the morning, when beginning my return journey, I had to send more than once to the kampong below to ask the men to come, because of their reluctance to carry burdens. We had to proceed slowly, and early in the afternoon reached the summit of the watershed, which naturally is not at its highest here, the elevation ascertained by boiling-point thermometer being 815 metres. At a temperature of 85° F., among shady trees, a short rest was very acceptable, and to get down the range proved quick work as the woods were not dense. Afterward we followed a path through tall grass over fallen trunks, crossing numerous gullies and rivulets. As darkness approached, clouds gathered threateningly and rain began to fall. It was really a pleasure to have the kapala of Tumingki meet us a couple of kilometres before arriving there. A man whom I had sent ahead to the river Tappin for the purpose of securing more baskets and to bring a woman to interpret the designs, had evidently told him about us.

CHAPTER XXIX

THE BALEI OR TEMPLE—A LITTLE KNOWN PART OF THE COUNTRY—A COURTEOUS MALAY—POWER OVER ANIMALS—NEGARA

THE kapala cleared the way with his parang, and just before dusk we arrived at the balei, a large structure which the people had taken as a permanent abode, having no houses and possessing ladangs near by. Many fires were burning inside, round which the families had gathered cooking rice, and my entire party also easily found room. The kapala at once sent out five men to gather the necessary coolies for the continuance of our journey the following day.

The carriers were slow in coming, and while waiting in the morning I catalogued four baskets which my messenger had brought from Tappin and a few more which I was able to buy here. The woman from Tappin, who accompanied my man, was even better informed than Dongiyak. She knew designs with remarkable certainty, and it was gratifying to be able to confirm information gathered before, also in two instances to correct errors. Many of the designs seemed familiar to the men standing around, for they, too, without being asked, would sometimes indicate the meaning correctly.

This done, I again inspected the balei, accompanied by the kapala who himself was a blian; he and the others were perfectly willing to give any information about customs and beliefs, although equally unable to do so. The dancing space in the middle was rectangular, about eight metres long, lying nearly east and west. It was about thirty centimetres lower than the remainder of the floor, on which I counted nineteen small rooms, or rather stalls. In the middle of the dancing place was a large ornamental stand made of wood, twice as high as a man, from which were hanging great quantities of stripped palm leaves. From the western part of the stand protruded upward a long narrow plank, painted with simple curved designs representing nagah, the great antoh, shaped like a serpent and provided with four short curved fangs stretched forward. The people could not be induced to sell the effigy because it was not yet one year old.

The country was uneven and heavy for travelling, or, as the carriers expressed it, the land was sakit (Malay for "ill"). There were more mountain ranges than I expected, rather low, though once we got a fine view of two quite impressive mountains. Here and there on the distant hillsides ladangs were seen and solitary houses could be discerned. On our arrival in the first kampong we were hospitably offered six young cocoanuts, considered a great delicacy even among white people. Although I do not much appreciate the sweetish, almost flavourless water of this fruit, they proved very acceptable to my men, as the day was intensely hot for Borneo.

At the kampong Belimbing, by taking out one of the walls which were constructed like stiff mats, I obtained a good room in the pasang grahan, but the difficulty about getting men increased. The kapala, or pumbakal, as this official is called in these parts, was obliging and friendly, but he had slight authority and little energy. He personally brought the men by twos and threes, finally one by one, and he worked hard. When finally we were able to start, still a couple of men short, he asked to be excused from accompanying me further, to which I readily assented. There were too many pumbakals who graced the expedition with their presence. I believe we had four that day who successively led the procession, generally with good intentions to be of assistance, but, in accordance with their dignity, carrying little or nothing, and receiving the same payment as the rest. However, it must be conceded that their presence helped to make an impression on the next kampong which was expected to furnish another gang of carriers.

We managed to travel along, and finally reached the last Dayak kampong, Bayumbong, consisting of the balei and a small house. The balei was of limited proportions, dark, and uninviting, so I put up my tent, which was easily done as the pumbakal and men were friendly and helpful. All the carriers were, of course, anxious to return, but as they were engaged to go to Kandangan I told them they would have to continue, promising, however, to pay for two days instead of one and to give them all rice in the evening. These people are like children, and in dealing with them a determined but accommodating ruling is necessary.

The journey was less rough than before, though we still passed gulches over which bamboo poles afforded passage for a single file, and soon the road began to be level. It was not more than four or five hours' walk to Kandangan, but rain began to fall and the men each took a leaf from the numerous banana trees growing along the road with which to protect themselves. On approaching the village we found two sheds some distance apart which had been built conveniently over the road for the comfort of travelling "inlanders." As the downpour was steady I deemed it wise to stop under these shelters, on account of the natives, if for no other reason, as they are unwilling carriers in rain.

The house of a Malay official was near by, and after a few minutes he came forth in the rain, a servant bringing a chair which he offered to me. Feeling hungry, I inquired if bananas were purchasable, but without immediate result. He was naturally curious to know where I came from, and having been satisfied in that respect he went back to his house, soon returning with bananas and a cup of tea. Hearing that I had been three weeks without mail and was anxious to have news of the war, he also brought me two illustrated Malay periodicals published in Amsterdam. Alas! they were half a year old, but nevertheless, among the illustrations were some I had not seen before. This was a worthy Malay and not unduly forward—he was too well-mannered for that.

The rain having abated somewhat we soon found ourselves in Kandangan, where the curiosity of Malays and Chinese was aroused by our procession. Neither the assistant-resident nor the controleur were at home, but the former was expected next morning. Many Malays, big and little, gathered in front of the pasang grahan,

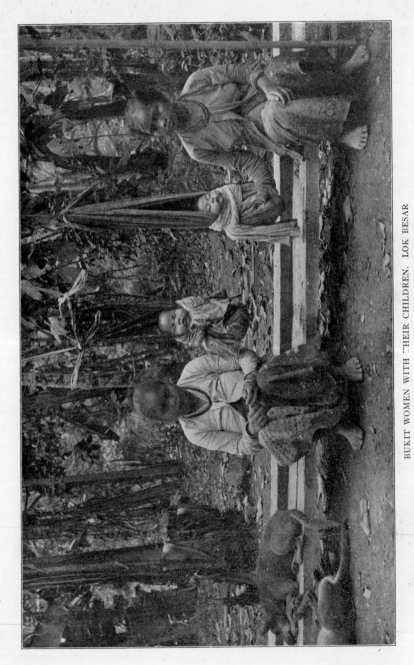

BUKIT WOMEN WITH THEIR CHILDREN. LOK BESAR

The peculiar cradles in which the infants gently swing were not observed in any other tribe on the journey

THE "ORDER" OF BERAUI, AND HIS WIFE, BOTH DUHOI. BERAUI, ON THE
SAMBA RIVER

where the man in charge could not be found, but a small boy started in search of him. After half-an-hour the rest of our party began to come in, and forty-five wet coolies with their damp burdens filled the ante-room of the pasang grahan, to the despair of the Malay custodian who belatedly appeared on the scene. Notwithstanding the unpleasantness of the crowded room I did not think it right to leave the poor carriers out in the rain, therefore had allowed them to remain. The burdens having been freed from the rattan and natural fibrous bands by which they had been carried, these wrappings—a load for two men—were disposed of by being thrown into the river. Gradually the place assumed an orderly aspect and Mr. Loing and I established ourselves in two quite comfortable rooms.

Through fortunate circumstances the assistant-resident, Mr. A. F. Meyer, was able to arrange to have our old acquaintance, the river-steamer *Otto*, to wait for us at Negara and take us to Bandjermasin. His wife had an interesting collection of live animals and birds from the surrounding country. She loved animals and possessed much power over them. A kitten of a wild cat of the jungle, obtained five days previously, was as tame as a domesticated specimen of the same age. She stroked the back of a hawk which was absolutely quiet without being tied or having its wings cut. He sat with his back toward us and as she stroked him merely turned his head, immediately resuming his former position. All the birds were in perfect plumage at that time, the month of November, and in fine condition.

We came to a number of beautiful rails, males and females, from the large marshes of the neighbourhood; the birds were busily running about, but at sight of her they stopped and emitted clacking notes. From the same marshes had been obtained many small brownish ducks with exquisitely shaded coats. The snake bird, with its long, straight, sharp beak and long, thin neck, she said was dangerous, and she teased him to thrust his head through the rails. Finally she took from a cage two musangs which were resting and pressed them against her chest. They were as tame as cats. It was curious to note that when walking they held their tails so that a loop was formed in the middle.

In Negara are many high-gabled houses, which I was told are Bandjermasin style; at all events, they form the original Malay architectural pattern in Borneo. The town is strongly Malay and famous for its boat-building. The gondola-like boats of ironwood that attract the attention of the stranger on his first visit to Bandjermasin, come from this place. Mosquitoes were troublesome in the surrounding marshes; nevertheless, I understand there is no malaria.

In this and similar sections in the vicinity of Bandjermasin it is noticeable that Malay women and girls whiten their faces on special occasions, doubtless in imitation of Chinese custom. The paint, called popor, is made from pulverised egg-shells mixed with water, and, for the finest quality, pigeons' egg-shells are utilised. Where there is much foreign influence Dayak women have adopted this fashion for festal occasions. At harvest time, when both

Dayak and Malay women wear their best garments, the faces of the women and the little girls are painted.

My expedition of three weeks had proved successful mainly on account of the unexpectedly well-preserved knowledge of decorative designs which I encountered among the Bukits. Otherwise they are slowly but surely yielding to the Malay influence to which they have been exposed for hundreds of years. Only the comparative inaccessibility of the country has prevented their complete absorption.

CHAPTER XXX

AN EXPEDITION TO THE KATINGAN RIVER—TATUING OF
THE ENTIRE BODY—THE GATHERING OF HONEY—A
PLEASANT INTERMEZZO—AN UNUSUALLY ARTISTIC PRO-
DUCTION—UP THE SAMBA RIVER—WITH INCOMPETENT
BOATMEN

ARRANGEMENTS were at once begun for another expedition, this time to the west of Bandjermasin. I
planned to ascend the Mendawei, or Katingan River, as
it is also called, and, if circumstances permitted, cross
over to the headwaters of the Sampit, returning by that
stream. Through the kind efforts of the resident, Mr.
H. J. Grijson, arrangements were made that would enable me to use the government's steam-launch *Selatan*
as far up the river as it is navigable, to Kuala Samba, and
in case necessity arose, to have it wait for my return.
This arrangement would save much time.

Accompanied by Mr. Loing, the surveyor, on the last
day of November I left Bandjermasin on the steamship
Janssens, which, en route for Singapore, was to call at
Sampit. There is always a large contingent of Malays
who with their families go on this steamer to and fro
between Borneo and the Malay Peninsula, where they
work on rubber and cocoanut plantations; out of their
earnings they buy the desires of their hearts—bicycles
and yellow shoes. Thus equipped they go back to Bandjermasin to enjoy themselves a few weeks, after which

the bicycles are sold and the erstwhile owners return to the scene of their labours to start afresh.

The controleur, Mr. H. P. Schouten, had just returned on the *Selatan* from a trip up the Katingan, and turned it over to my use. When the coaling had been done and our goods taken on board, the strong little boat lay deep, but the captain said it was all right. He was the same able djuragan of two years before. Having received from the controleur letters to the five native officials located on the Katingan, we departed, and the following morning arrived at the mouth of the river. At first the country was very thinly inhabited, because the banks are too low to encourage settlement. As hitherto noted the country bordering on the lower portions of the great rivers is populated by Malays exclusively, and here their territory stretches almost to Kasungan. The remainder of the riparian lands is occupied by Katingans. There is some slight difference in the language spoken by those who live on the middle part, from Kasungan to Bali (south of Kuala Samba), and those who from Bali northward occupy the rest of the watercourse. They are termed by the Malays Lower and Upper Katingans. Those of the first category appeared to be of medium size and inclined to stoutness; on the upper stretches of the river they are taller. These and other differences may be due in a measure to tribal changes brought about by head-hunting raids. It is known that there was an influx of Ot-Danums from the Samba on account of such raids. While all Katingans eat snakes and large lizards, the upper ones do not eat rusa but the lower ones do.

Their total number is estimated to be about 6,000. In 1911–1912 this river was visited by cholera and small-pox, which reduced the population by 600 and caused the abandonment of some kampongs.

Under favourable circumstances one may travel by prahu to Kuala Samba, our first goal, in sixteen days, the return journey occupying half that time. On reaching Kasungan the river was not quite two metres deep, dimming our chances of proceeding further with the steam-launch. The djuragan put up his measuring rod on the beach, for unless the water rose he would have to go one day down stream. The prospect was not pleasing. The under kapala of the district, a native official whose title for the sake of convenience is always abbreviated to the "onder," at once exerted himself in search of a large boat belonging to a Malay trader, supposed to be somewhere in the neighbourhood, and a young Dutchman who recently had established himself here as a missionary was willing to rent me his motor-boat to tow it.

After several days of preparation, the river showing no sign of rising, we started in an unusually large prahu which was provided with a kind of deck made of palm-leaf mats and bamboo, slightly sloping to each side. It would have been quite comfortable but for the petroleum smoke from the motor-boat, which was sickening and made everything dirty.

In 1880, when Controleur W. J. Michielsen visited the Katingan and Samba Rivers, the kampongs consisted of "six to ten houses each, which are lying in a row along the river bank and shaded by many fruit trees, especially cocoanut palms and durians." A similar description would serve to-day. The large communal house as known in most parts of Borneo does not seem to obtain here. Communal houses of small size were in use ten years previously and are still found on the Upper Samba. Their gradual disappearance may be explained by the fact that the government, as I was informed, does not encourage the building of communal houses.

Whatever the reason, at the present time the dwelling is a more or less flimsy structure, built with no thought of giving access to fresh air, and sometimes no provision is made for the escape of smoke from the fireplace. But the people are very hospitable; they gladly received us in their houses, and allowed me, for purposes of ventilation, to demolish temporarily part of the unsubstantial wall, which consisted of bark or stiff mats. The high ladder is generally provided with a railing leaning outward at either side.

The Katingans are shy, kind-hearted natives, the great majority of them being unusually free from skin disease. No illness was apparent. With some of the Lower Katingans the calf of the leg was below normal size. This was the case with three women in Pendahara, and also with a blian who otherwise was a stout man. All the men have a large representation of the full moon tatued on the calf of the leg, following the custom of the Ot-Danums, Murungs, and Siangs. As far as I ascended the river the Upper Katingans rarely have more tatuing than this, but the Lower Katingans are elaborately ornamented, chest and arms being covered with illustrations of familiar objects. Several old men, now dead, had their bodies, even their backs, legs, and faces, covered with tatu marks, and one thus decorated was said still to be living.

Near the kampong Pendahara, where we camped the first night, were many of the majestic tapang trees which I first noticed on the Barito. In the calm evening after a light shower, with the moon almost full, their tall stems and beautiful crowns were reflected in the placid water. The Katingans guard and protect these trees because they are the abode of bees, and when the Malays cut them down the Dayaks are indignant. Both honey and wax are gathered, the latter to be sold. The nest is reached in the customary manner by a ladder of sharpened bamboo pegs driven into the rather soft wood as the man ascends. The gathering is done at night, an assistant bearing a torch made of bark and filled with damar or wax. The native first smears himself with honey in order that the bees shall not sting him; when he reaches the deposit a large bark bucket is hoisted up and filled. In lowering it the honey sometimes disappears, my informant said, because antoh is very fond of it.

About noon, as we were passing a ladang near Bali, we heard the beating of a gong, also weird singing by a woman. It was evident that a ceremony of some kind was in progress, probably connected with funeral observances, so I ordered a halt. As we lay by many people gathered on the top of the steep bank. We learned that an old woman had died and that the ceremonies were being performed in her honour. I climbed the ladder and found in front of me a house on poles, simply constructed, as they always are at the ladangs. Several of the men wore chavats; an elderly female blian sang continuously, and a fire was burning outside.

Ascending the ladder of the house I entered a dingy room into which the light came sparingly. In a corner many women were sitting silently. Near them stood one of the beautiful red baskets for which the Katingans higher up the river are famous. As I proceeded a little further an extremely fine carved casket met my astonished eyes. Judging from its narrowness the deceased, who had been ill for a long time, must have been very thin when she passed away, but the coffin, to which the cover had been fastened with damar, was of excellent proportions and symmetrical in shape. The material was a lovely white wood of Borneo, on which were drawn large round flowers on graceful vines, done in a subdued light red colour procured from a pigment found in the earth. The effect was magnificent, reminding me of French tapestries. Two diminutive and unfinished mats were lying on the cover, symbolising clothing for the deceased, and tufts of long, beautiful grass had been tied to the top at either end. The coffin was to be placed on a platform in the utan. Its name in Katungan is bákan rúni; (bákan = form, exterior; rúni = dead person)

To see such an artistic production was worth a great deal of trouble. Usually this and similar work is made by several working in unison, who co-operate to obtain the best result in the shortest time. I was gratified when they agreed to make an exact copy for me, to be ready on my

return from up country. When one of the men consented
to pose before the camera his wife fled with ludicrous pre-
cipitation. A dwarf was photographed, forty years old
and unmarried, whose height was 1.13 metres.

I was about to leave when the people began to be-
have in a boisterous manner. Men caught firebrands
and beat with them about the feet of the others. Some
cut mats in pieces, ignited them, and struck with those.
A woman came running out of the house with a piece of
burning mat and beat me about my feet and ankles (my
trousers and shoes were supposed to be white) and then
went after others, all in good humour and laughingly.
She next exchanged firebrands with a man, and both
struck at each other repeatedly. This same custom
is used at funerals with the Ot-Danums on the Samba,
and the explanation given in both tribes is that the
mourners want to forget their grief.

After distributing pieces of chewing-tobacco to all
present, which seemed to please them much, I left the
entertaining scene. In the afternoon we arrived at
a small kampong, Tevang Karangan, (tevang = inlet;
karangan = a bank of coarse sand or pebbles) where Upper
Katingans appeared for the first time. No Malays live
here, but there is much intermixture with Ot-Danums.
The people were without rice, and edible roots from the
jungle were lying in the sun to dry. The cemetery was
close at hand in the outskirts of the jungle, where little
houses could be seen consisting simply of platforms on
four poles with roofs of palm-leaf mats, each containing
one, two, or three coffins. It is impossible to buy skulls

from the Dayaks on account of their fear that the insult may be avenged by the ghost of the original owner, through the infliction of misfortunes of various kinds—illness, loss of crops, etc. According to their belief, punishment would not descend upon the stranger who abstracted a human bone from a coffin, but upon the natives who permitted the theft. Moreover, they believe they have a right to kill the intruder; the bone must be returned and a pig killed as a sacrifice to the wandering liao of the corpse. But the case is somewhat different with slaves, who up to some thirty years ago were commonly kept in these districts, and whose bodies after death were disposed of separately from those of free people.

Kuala Samba is quite a large kampong situated at the junction of the Samba with the Katingan River, and inhabited chiefly by the Bakompai, a branch of the Malays. Our large boat had to remain here until we returned from our expedition up the Samba, the main tributary of the river and inhabited by Ot-Danums who are called Duhoi, their proper name in these parts. I desired to start immediately and the "onder" of the place, as well as the pumbakal, at once set to work chasing for prahus, but things moved slowly and people seemed to take their own time about obeying the authorities.

Not until nine o'clock next day could we leave, and I was glad it was no later. The prahus in these regions are large and comfortable, with a bamboo covering in the bottom. They probably originated with the Bakompai, but the Duhoi also make them. At five o'clock it was thought best to camp at the lonely house of a Kahayan, recently immigrated here, whose wife was a Duhoi woman. As usual I had to remove part of the wall to get air, the family sleeping in the next room. In the small hours of the morning, by moonlight, two curious heads appeared in the doorway, like silhouettes, to observe me, and as the surveillance became annoyingly persistent I shortened the exercises I usually take.

At the first kampong prahus and paddlers were changed, and on a rainy day we arrived at a small kampong, Kuluk Habuus, where I acquired some unusually interesting carved wooden objects called kapatongs, connected with the religious life of the Duhoi and concerning which more will be told presently. As a curious fact may be mentioned that a Kahayan living here had a full, very strong growth of beard. A few more of the Kahayans, one in Kuala Kapuas for instance, are known to be similarly endowed by nature although not in the same degree as this one. The families hospitably vacated their rooms in our favour, and a clean new rattan mat was spread on the floor. At Tumbang Mantike, on this river, there is said to be much iron ore of good quality, from which formerly even distant tribes derived their supplies.

I had been told that a trip of a few hours would bring us to the next kampong, but the day proved to be a very long one. There were about five kihams to pass, all of considerable length though not high. It soon became evident that our men, good paddlers as they were, did not know how to overcome these, hesitating and making up for their inefficiency by shouting at the top of their voices. However insignificant the stream, they yelled as if passing a risky place. Sunset came and still the kampong was—djau (far). Mr. Loing had gone in our small prahu with four of our best men to finish the map-making, if possible, before darkness set in.

The light of day faded, though not so quickly as the books represent, but soon it was as dark as possible before the appearance of the waning moon which would not be visible for several hours. I had let Mr. Loing have my lamp, so I lit a candle. It was not a pleasant experience, with clumsy stupid men who, however, did their best, all finally taking to the water, wading and pushing the boat, constantly emitting loud, hoarse cries to encourage themselves; and thus we progressed little by little. What with the faint light of the candle, the constant rush of water, and the noise of the rapids, though not dangerous in the day time, the situation demanded calmness. More-over, there was the possibility of an overflow of the river, which often happens, caused by rains above. I thought of the Kenyahs of the Bulungan—if I only had them now. After an hour and a half of this exasperating sort of prog-ress we came to smooth water, but even here the men lost time by running into snags which they ought to have seen, because I had gotten my hurricane lamp from Mr. Loing whom we had overtaken. One of the men was holding it high up in the bow, like the Statue of Liberty in New York harbour.

There were only three or four houses at the kampong where we arrived at nine o'clock, but people kindly per-mitted us to occupy the largest. The men were allowed an extra ration of rice on account of their exertions since eight o'clock in the morning, as well as some maize that I had bought, and all came into the room to cook at the fireplace. Besides Mr. Loing and myself all our baggage was there, and the house, built on high poles, was very shaky. The bamboo floor gave way in a disagreeable manner, and it did not seem a remote possibility for it to fall, though the genial lady of the manor, who went away herself, assured us that the house was strong. I did not feel thoroughly comfortable until the "onder" and the thirteen men had finished their cooking and gone elsewhere to camp. When all was quiet and we could go to sleep it was twelve o'clock.

Early in the morning Mr. Loing went back in the small prahu to take up the map where he had been compelled to quit on account of the darkness. In the meantime I had opportunity to receive a man who had been reported to me the previous night as wanting assistance because of a wound on his head. Knowing that the Dayaks are always ready to seize an opportunity to obtain medicine, even when they are well, I postponed examining into his case. He had merely a scratch on his forehead—not even a swelling.

CHAPTER XXXI

AMONG THE DUHOI (OT-DANUMS)—RICH COLLECTIONS—
THE KAPATONGS—THE BATHING OF DAYAK INFANTS—
CHRISTMAS EVE—THE FLYING BOAT—MARRIAGE CERE-
MONIES

As we approached the kampong Kuala Braui, our next
objective, the men in our prahus began yelling in time,
in a manner surprisingly like a college yell. We were
received at the landing float by the "onder" of the place,
a nervous and shy but intelligent looking Duhoi. Pa-
jamas graced his tall form as an outward sign that he was
more than an ordinary Dayak, and he wore the same suit
every day for a week without washing it. He spoke very
few Malay words, which made intercourse with him difficult. Very gentle and retiring, by those unacquainted
with the Dayaks he would be regarded as unlikely to
possess head-hunting proclivities; nevertheless, twenty
years previous to my visit, this same man avenged members of his family who had been deprived of their heads
by Penyahbongs, killing two of the band and preserving
their heads. Ten years before he had presented them to
Controleur Baren on the Kayan River, thus depriving
me of the chance I had hoped for on my arrival.

The small kampong on the river bank, which here is
over twenty metres high and very steep, is new, and a
primitive pasang grahan was in course of erection. Six
men were much entertained by the novel work of putting

up my tent and received tobacco as remuneration. The place lies near an affluent from the north, called Braui, which is more difficult of ascent than the Samba on account of its many kiams. The kapala of the kampong, with two prahus, had ascended it in twenty days. The Dayaks told me that if they wanted gold they were able to wash much in these rivers when the water is low.

I heard here of large congregations of wild pigs, up to 500 or 1,000. When the herds, called dundun, have eaten all the fruit at one place they move to another, feeding and marching, following one leader. They can be heard at a great distance, and there is time to seek safety by climbing a tree or running. When hunting pigs in the customary way, with dogs and spears, men have been killed by these animals, though the victims are never eaten. A fine rusa with large horns was killed one day when crossing the river, and I preserved the head. It seemed to me to have shorter hair on the back and sides than this deer usually has, and was larger. The flesh tasted extremely well, in fact much better than that of the ordinary variety. During our stay here, in December, a strong wind blew almost every day, late in the afternoon, not always bringing rain, and quite chilly after sunset.

When Schwaner made his memorable exploration in 1847 he did not come up the Samba, but ascended the Katingan River, returning to Western Borneo over the mountains that bear his name. Controleur Michielsen, in 1880, was the first European to visit the Samba River, and since then it has been ignored by explorers. It is part of a large region occupied by the Ot-Danums, a name which signifies people living at the sources (ot) of the rivers (danum = water, river). They are found chiefly around the headwaters of the Kapuas and the Kahayan, and on the Samba and Braui. Some also live on the upper tributaries to the Katingan, for instance on the Hiran. On all these rivers they may number as many as 5,000, about 1,200 of which should be located on the Samba and the Braui. The last figures are fairly correct, but the first ones are based only on information derived from native sources.

On the Samba, where I met the Ot-Danums, they are known as Duhoi, a name applied by themselves and other tribes. They are still in a primitive condition, though in outward appearance beginning to show the effect of foreign influence While a few wear chavats and sometimes becoming rattan caps, nearly all cut their hair, and they no longer have sumpitans. Higher up the river is a Malay kampong consisting of settlers from the Western Division. Occasional traders also bring about inevitable changes, though as yet few of these Dayaks speak Malay.

The Kahayans who live to the east of them always liked to come to the Samba, often marrying Duhoi wives, and they also exert an influence. In intellect they are superior to the Duhoi as well as in knowledge of worldly affairs, in that respect resembling the Malays, though they have none of their objectionable qualities. One or two of them are generally present in a kampong, and I always found them useful because they speak Malay well besides being truthful and reliable. Some of these are converts to Christianity through the efforts of the Protestant mission on the Kahayan River, which has begun to extend its activity to the Samba by means of such Kahayans.

I prevailed on the "onder" to call the people from three kampongs above, promising presents of rice. He wrote the order himself in Arabic letters and sent it on, and late the following day twenty-five Duhoi arrived, among them four women and several children. Many showed indications of having had smallpox, not in a scarred face, but by the loss of an eye; one man was totally blind from the same cause. In order to induce them to dance I bought a domestic pig, which was brought from the ladang and in the customary way was left on the ground in the middle of the dancing place. Four men attended to the gongs which had unusually fine tones.

The women were persuaded to come forward with difficulty. As I expected, they were like bundles of cloth, exhibiting Malay innovations, and the dance was uninteresting, each woman keeping her position in a stationary circle. There was not much life in the dancing of the men either, each performing at his place in a similar circle, with some movements resembling the most common form of dancing hitherto described. Finally, one whose long hair and attire, an ancient short shirt, betrayed him as belonging to the old school, suddenly stepped forward, drew his parang, and began to perform a war dance, swinging himself gracefully in a circle. Another man was almost his equal, and these two danced well around the babi which was lying at the foot of two thin upright bamboo poles; to the top of one of these a striped cloth had been tied.

This meeting was followed by friendly dealings with the Dayaks of the kampongs above, who began to visit me. Silent and unobtrusive, they often seated themselves before my tent, closely observing my movements, especially at meal time, eager to get the tin that soon would be empty. A disagreeable feature, however, was that the natives often brought mosquitoes with them, and when they began to slap themselves on arms and legs their absence would have been more acceptable than their company. But each day they offered for sale objects of great interest and variety. Several beautifully engraved wah-wah (long armed monkey) bones, serving as handles for women's knives, are worthy of mention, one of which might be termed exquisite in delicate execution of design. Admirable mats were made by the tribe, but the designs proved perplexing to interpret, as knowledge on the subject seems to be lost. The difficulty about an interpreter was solved when the "onder's" clerk returned from a brief absence; he was an intelligent and trustworthy Kayan who spoke Malay well, had been a Christian for six years, but adopted Islam when he married a Bakompai wife. Compared with the retiring "onder," who, though a very good man, seemed to feel the limitations of his position, this Kahayan appeared more like a man of the world.

I made a large collection of kapatongs (in Kahayan, hapatong), which here, and in less degree on the Katingan, I found more abundant than in any region of Borneo visited. These interesting objects are carved representations of a good antoh, or of man, bird, or animal which good antohs have entered, and which, therefore, are believed to protect their owners. When the carving has been finished the blian invokes a beneficent antoh to take it in possession, by dancing and singing one or two nights and by smearing blood on it from the sacrifice of a fowl, pig, or a water-buffalo—formerly often taken from a slave. As with a person, so with a kapatong; nobody is permitted to step over it lest the good antoh which resides in it should become frightened and flee.

Kapatongs are made from ironwood; they are of various kinds and serve many purposes. The larger ones, which appear as crude statues in many kampongs of Southern Borneo, more rarely on the Mahakam, are supposed to be attendants on the souls of the dead and were briefly described on page 116.

The smaller kapatongs are used for the protection of the living and all their earthly belongings or pursuits. These images and their pedestals are usually carved from one block, though the very small ones may be made to stand inside of an upright piece of bamboo. Some kapatongs are placed in the ladang to protect the crops, others in the storehouse or inside the baskets where rice or food is kept. The monkey, itself very predatory on the rice fields, is converted into an efficient watchman in the form of its image, which is considered an excellent guardian of boiled rice that may be kept over from one meal to the next.

For protection at night the family may have a number of images, preferably seven, placed upright and tied together, standing near the head of the bed; a representation of the tiger-cat is placed on top of it all, for he impersonates a strong, good antoh who guards man night and day. From the viewpoint of the Katingans the tiger-cat is even more powerful than the nagah. When cholera or smallpox is apprehended, some kapatongs of fair size are left standing outside the room or at the landing places of the prahus. Images representing omen birds guard the house, but may also be carried on a journey in a basket which is placed near the head when a man is sleeping in a prahu or on land. A kapatong of one particular omen bird is thus capable of allaying any fear if real omen birds or snakes should pass in front of the boat.

On head-hunting expeditions kapatongs were of prime importance. Smeared with blood, they were taken along for protection and guidance, and afterward were returned to the room. Some of them are very curious; a favourite one represents a pregnant woman, the idea being that a woman with a child is a good watcher, as the infant cries and keeps her awake. That the child is not yet born is of no consequence. In my possession is a kapatong of the head-hunters which represents a woman in the act of bearing a child. Among the Dayaks the woman is regarded as the more alert and watchful; at night it is she who perceives danger and thrusts her hand against her husband's side to arouse him.

When feasts occur kapatongs, etc., are taken outside the house to partake of blood from the animal or (formerly) the slave sacrificed. They are supposed to drink it and are smeared with it. When important they are never sold, but are transmitted as heirlooms from father to son. They passed in a circuit among brothers, remaining three to five years with each, and were the cause of much strife, brother having been known to kill brother if deprived of his kapatong.

Many of those which came into my possession showed distinct traces of the application of blood. Some had necklaces around the necks as a sign that they had received human blood. A few of these were later estimated by an intelligent Dayak to be two hundred years old. At the time of purchase I was struck with the fact that the Ot-Danums were parting with objects of great importance in their religious life. One reason is that the young generation no longer practises head-hunting, which necessitated the use of a great number of kapatongs. The people are gradually losing faith in them.

These Duhoi were curiously varying in their physical aspects; some were tall, like the "onder," others of medium size; some had hooked noses, others turned up noses. The wife of the "onder" had unusually light skin, but there was no indication of a mixture of white blood. Their temperament is peaceful and gentle, and, according to the Kahayan clerk, who had been here ten years, they are truthful. Most of those that were measured came from the kampongs above, one of which is only two or three hours away. Several men had their

A DUHOI AND HIS FAMILY.   BERAUI, SAMBA RIVER

This type of bygone times danced a head-hunting dance for my benefit

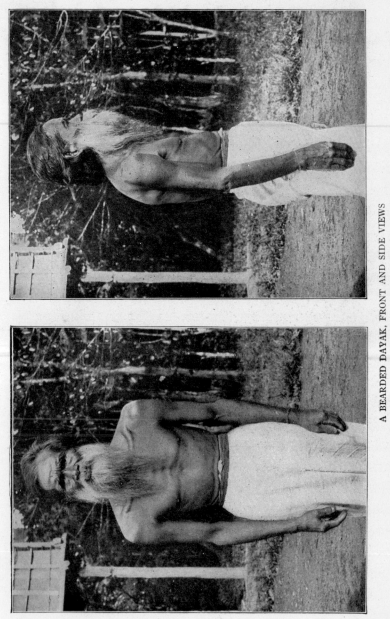

A BEARDED DAYAK, FRONT AND SIDE VIEWS

A full-bearded native is a most unusual spectacle in Borneo. This Kayan lived at Kuluk Habuus, Samba River

foreheads shaved in a manner similar to the Chinese, a straight line from ear to ear forming the hair limit. I observed the same fashion with the Upper Katingans, and in rare cases also with the Kayans and Kenyahs. They make fire by drilling one upright stick into another lying on the ground. Seven is their sacred number. Formerly the kampongs elected a kapala for an indefinite period. If he was satisfactory he might remain a long time. At present the native kapala of the district makes the appointment.

Among my friends here were the kapala of the kampong and his wife. She was an interesting woman, very intelligent, with a slender but splendid figure, and her face was curiously Mongolian. She had lost an eye by smallpox, but there was so much light and vivacity in the brown one she had left that the missing organ was forgotten. At first sternly refusing to face the camera, after receiving chocolate like the rest both she and her husband wanted to be photographed.

More than once I have seen the Dayak father here and elsewhere take the youngest baby to the river to bathe. As soon as the navel is healed, about eight days after birth, the infant is immersed, usually twice a day, before seven o'clock in the morning and at sunset. The temperature of the river water here in the morning was 72° F. It is astonishing how the helpless little nude being, who can neither walk nor talk, remains absolutely quiet while being dipped under the cold water again and again. The father holds it in a horizontal position for immersion, which lasts only a few moments, but which undoubtedly would evoke lusty cries from a white child. Between the plunges, which are repeated at least three times, with his hand he strokes water from the little body which after a few seconds is dipped again. It seems almost cruel, but not a dissenting voice is heard. The bath over he takes the child into his arms, ascends the ladder of the river bank and carries it home as silent as when it went forth. Sometimes one may hear children cry from being cross, but as a rule they are charming.

Monkeys, including the orang-utan, are eaten, but not the crocodile nor the tiger-cat. In accordance with the prevailing Dayak custom men and women eat at the same time. If they choose, women may accompany fishing or hunting expeditions if not far away, but when the game is wild ox or rhinoceros they are not allowed to take part. When there is an overflow of the river one cannot go hunting, nor if one should fall at the start, nor if the rattan bag should drop when the man slings it on his back, or if anybody sneezes when about to leave the house. If when going out on an errand one stubs his toe against the threshold, he must wait an hour. Having started on a fishing or hunting expedition nobody is permitted to go back home; should this be done the enterprise would be a failure for the others; nor should the dogs, on a pig hunt, be called in while on a ladang lest monkeys and deer eat the paddi. When about to undertake a journey of more than four or five days' duration one must abstain from eating snake or turtle, and if a pregnant woman eats these reptiles the child will look like them. Should she eat fruit that has fallen to the ground, the child will be still-born. The same prohibition applies to lizards.

Up to twenty years ago the Duhoi and the Katingans made head-hunting raids on each other. It was the custom to take a little flesh from the arm or leg of the victim, which was roasted and eaten. Before starting on such an expedition the man must sleep separate from his wife seven days; when going pig-hunting the separation is limited to one day. On the Upper Samba the custom still prevails of drinking tuak from human skulls. This was related to me by the "onder" of Kasungan, a trustworthy man who had himself seen it done.

A wide-awake kapala from one of the kampongs above was of excellent service in explaining the purposes of the ethnological objects I purchased. About articles used by women he was less certain, but he gave me much valuable information, though it was impossible to keep him as long as I desired because he felt anxious about the havoc rusa and monkeys might make with his paddi fields. At five o'clock of an afternoon I had finished, and in spite of a heavy shower the kapala left to look after his paddi, with a night journey of six hours before him. These people are satisfied with little, and he was happy to receive, besides rice and money, a quantity of cocoanut oil and some empty tin cans thrown in.

During this busy day the thought occurred to me that the night was Christmas eve, the great festival in Scandinavian countries, and I had made no preparation for a better meal, having neither time nor means. In fact, it so happened that I had rather less than usual. Nevertheless, the day had passed happily, as I accomplished much and acquired interesting information, for instance, about the flying prahu which I had secured. It was about half a metre long, and this and similar models seem to be quite an institution in the southern parts of Borneo. The Duhoi and the Katingans use the contrivance for curing disease, though not in the way we should expect, by carrying away the disorder, but by making a present of the prahu to a good antoh to facilitate his journey.

The name of the flying prahu is menáma, in Katingan, melambong. The more or less wavy carvings of the edge represent the beach. On board are several wooden images: The great hornbill which carries the prahu along and steers it; the tiger-cat, which guards it; the gong and two blanga (valuable urns), to which are added a modernism in the shape of a rifle—all are there ready to drive away the bad antoh which caused the illness. To a pole—or rather a combination of two poles—are tied two rudely made wooden figures, one above the other, representing, the one below, the djuragan or skipper (tiháng); the one above, the master of the "sails" (únda).

When a Duhoi is very ill and able to pay the blian five florins, he promises a good antoh to give him a menáma if he will make him well. The contrivance is then made and the necessary ceremonies performed to the end that its purpose shall be fulfilled. In the presence of many persons, the afflicted man lying on his mat, the blian dances in the room holding the prahu on his hands, the left at the bow, and swerving it to left and to right; he sings at the same time but there is no other music. On three consecutive nights this performance is continued for about an hour, near the door, with an eye to the ship's departure, and although it does not disappear it is believed to have accomplished its mission.

The Duhoi are polygamous, as are the Kahayans. According to a rough estimate, one-third of the people have one wife, one-third two, and one-third three. If a girl declines the suitor on whose behalf the father acts, she is not forced and the matter is closed. Should she agree, then the price must first be determined, and is paid in goods, gongs, cattle, domestic pigs, water-buffaloes, etc. Really poor people are not found here, and the least amount a man pays for his wife is two gongs, which are procured from the Malay trader.

About sunset people gather for the marriage ceremony. The couple sit on one gong. A water-buffalo, pig, or fowl having been sacrificed, the blian sings and smears blood on navel, chest, and forehead of the pair. On rising to go to their room the bridegroom beats seven times upon the gong on which they were sitting, and before he enters the door he strikes the upper lintel three times, shouting loudly with each blow. Food is brought there, and while the door is left open the newly wedded eat meat and a stew of nangka seasoned with red pepper and salt, the guests eating at the same time. After the meal the bridegroom gives everybody tuak, and people go home the same evening unless they become drunk, which often happens. The young married couple remain one year with the bride's parents.

CHAPTER XXXII

AGRICULTURAL PURSUITS—FACTS ABOUT ULU-OTS, THE
WILD MEN OF BORNEO—TAKING LEAVE OF THE INTER-
ESTING DUHOI—A VISIT TO THE UPPER KATINGANS—
DANCING—FRIENDLY NATIVES—DOWN THE KATINGAN
RIVER

WHEN about to make a new ladang one fowl is sacrificed in the morning and the blood, with the usual addition of rice, is thrown up in the air by the husband or
wife as a present to antoh, the meat being reserved for
home consumption.   On arrival at the selected place they
carry the sharpening stone some distance into the utan
where a portion of the same mixture is applied to it.   A
few weeks are devoted to cutting down the jungle, and
then about a month must pass before the felled trees,
bushes, and vines are dry enough to burn.

On the day chosen for burning the wood a winnowing
tray, on which the outline of a human form has been
crudely drawn with charcoal, is hung in the house.   The
picture represents a good antoh named Putjong and he is
solicited to make the wind blow.   When starting the
fire every one yells "hoi," thereby calling the winds.
One day, or even a shorter time, may suffice to burn the
accumulations on the cleared space, and when the work is
finished all the participants must bathe.

A simple house is then erected for occupancy while
doing the necessary work incident to the raising of crops.
The work of clearing the ground is immediately begun

and completed in three or four weeks. Then comes planting of the paddi preceded by a sacrifice of pig or fowl. The blood, with the usual addition, is presented to antoh and also smeared on the seed, which may amount to ten baskets full. All the blood having been disposed of in this manner, the meat is put over the fire to cook, and at the noon-day meal is eaten with boiled rice.

In their agricultural pursuits people help each other, taking different fields in turn, and at planting time thirty men may be engaged making holes in the ground with long sticks, some of which may have rattles on one end, a relic of former times, but every one uses the kind he prefers. After them follow an equal number of women, each carrying a small basket of paddi which she drops with her fingers into the holes, where it remains uncovered. They do not plant when rain is falling. After planting is finished, usually in one day, they repair to the kampong, have their evening meal, and drink tuak until midnight.

In five months the paddi is ready for cutting—a very busy time for the people. There are perhaps fifty ladangs and all must be harvested. Husband, wife, and children all work, and the family may have to labour by themselves many weeks before helpers come. In the afternoon of the day previous to commencing harvest work the following ceremony is performed, to provide for which the owner and his wife have brought new rice from the ladang as well as the kapatongs, which in the number of two to five have been guarding the crop.

Inside the room a couple of winnowing trays are laid on the floor and on these are placed the kapatongs in recumbent position, axes, parangs, the small knives used for cutting paddi and other knives, spears for killing pigs as well as those for fish, fish-hooks and lines, the sharpening stone and the hammer used in making parangs and other iron utensils. The guardians of the ladang and the implements are to be regaled with new paddi.

Blood of pig and fowls mixed with new rice having been duly offered to antoh, the mixture is smeared on the kapatongs and implements and a small quantity is also placed on a plate near the trays. Here also stands a dish of boiled rice and meat, the same kind of food which is eaten later by the family. The owner with wife and children having concluded their meal, all others present and as many as care to come are welcome to partake of new rice and meat and to drink tuak.

On the following day they go to the ladang to cut paddi, but barely half the number that took part in the feast assist in the work. The first rice spear that is cut is preserved to be taken home and tied underneath the roof outside the door. This is done in order to prevent birds, monkeys, rusa, or babi from eating the paddi. At the ladang rice is boiled, and on this occasion the family and their guests eat at the same time. When the first baskets of new paddi arrive at the storehouse and the grain is poured out on the floor, a little blood from a fowl sacrificed is smeared on it after the necessary offering to antoh has been thrown up into the air.

Upon the death of a man who was well-to-do, the body is kept for a period of seven days in the coffin, within the family dwelling-house, but for a poor man one day and night is long enough. Many people gather for the funeral. There is little activity in the day time, but at night the work, as the natives call it, is performed, some weeping, others dancing. When the room is large the feast is held in the house, otherwise, outside. Fire is kept burning constantly during the night, but not in the day time. Many antohs are supposed to arrive to feast on the dead man. People are afraid of these supernatural associations but not of the departed soul. Formerly, when erecting a funeral house for an important man, an attendant in the next life was provided for him by placing a slave, alive, in the hole dug for one of the upright posts, the end of the post being set directly over him.

On the Samba I found myself in close proximity to regions widely spoken of elsewhere in Borneo as being inhabited by particularly wild people, called Ulu-Ots: (ulu=men; ot=at the headwaters). Their habitats are the mountainous regions in which originate the greatest rivers of Borneo, the Barito, the Kapuas (western), and the Mahakam, and the mountains farther west, from whence flow the Katingan, the Sampit, and the Pembuang, are also persistently assigned to these ferocious natives. They are usually believed to have short tails and to sleep in trees. Old Malays may still be found who tell of fights they had forty or more years ago with these wild men. The Kahayans say that the Ulu-Ots are cannibals, and have been known to force old men and women to climb trees and hang by their hands to the branches until sufficiently exhausted to be shaken down and killed. The flesh is roasted before being eaten.

They know nothing of agriculture and to them salt and lombok are non-existent. Few of them survive. On the authority of missionaries there are some three hundred such savages at the headwaters of the Kahayan, who are described as very Mongolian in appearance, with oblique eyes and prominent cheekbones, and who sleep in trees.

They are considered inveterate head-hunters, and the skulls of people killed by them are used as drinking-vessels. Controleur Michielsen, who in his report devotes two pages of hearsay to them, concludes thus: "In the Upper Katingan for a long time to come it will be necessary to exercise a certain vigilance at night against attacks of the Ulu-Ot head-hunters." A civilised Kahayan who, twelve years previous to my visit, came upon one unawares at the headwaters of the Samba, told me that the man carried in his right hand a sampit, in his left a shield, and his parang was very large. He wore a chavat made of fibre, and in his ear-lobes were inserted large wooden disks; his skin was rather light and showed no tatuing; the feet were unusually broad, the big toe turned inward, and he ran on his toes, the heels not touching the ground.

Without precluding the possibility, although remote, of some small, still unknown tribe, it seems safe to assume that Ulu-Ot is simply a collective name for several mountain tribes of Central Borneo with whom we already have made acquaintance—the Penyahbongs, Saputans, Bukits, and Punans. Of these the last two are nomads, the first named have recently been induced to become agriculturists, and the Saputans some fifty years ago were still in an unsettled state. The "onder" at Braui confirmed this opinion when telling me of the fight he and thirty other Duhoi once had with Penyahbongs from whom he captured two heads—for they are Ulu-Ots, he said.

Before all my things were cleared away from my camping-place and taken to the prahus, the kapala and three women, one of them his wife, came and seated themselves in a row close together in a squatting position. With the few words of Malay he knew he explained that the women wanted to say good-bye. No doubt it was their way, otherwise they have no greetings. At the landing float the "onder" and his Kahayan assistant were present to see us off. When leaving I was on the point of wishing I might return some day to the unsophisticated Duhoi.

On our arrival at Kuala Samba we found ourselves in a different atmosphere. The Bakompai, although affable, are inquisitive and aggressive, and do not inspire one with confidence. The cheerful old Kahayan who lived on board our big prahu to guard it had just one measure of rice left, and was promptly given more rations. On account of the low water and the difficulties attending my use of the *Selatan* it had long been evident that I should have to give up my tour to the head of the Katingan River, but before returning I desired to make the ascent as far as to the first renowned kiham in order to see more of the Upper Katingans.

My prahu leaked so badly that we had to bail it out constantly, and the men were the worst in my experience, lazy and very inefficient, only one of them being strong and agile. Not until eight o'clock in the evening did we reach our destination, the kampong Buntut Mangkikit. In beautiful moonlight I put up my tent on the clearing along the river bank in front of the houses, perhaps for the last time in a long period. The roar of the rapids nearly two kilometres distant was plainly audible and soothing to the nerves, reminding me of the subdued sound of remote waterfalls, familiar to those who have travelled in Norway. However, the kiham at this time was not formidable and comparatively few have perished there, but many in the one below, which, though lower in its fall and very long, is full of rocks. The nights here were surprisingly cool, almost cold, and the mornings very chilly.

A Kahayan was the only person about the place who could speak Malay. The kapala presented the unusual spectacle of a man leaning on a long stick when walking, disabled from wasting muscles of the legs. I have seen a Lower Katingan who for two years had suffered in this way, his legs having little flesh left, though he was able to move. The kapala was a truthful and intelligent man who commanded respect. His wife was the greatest of the four blians here, all women; male blians, as usual, being less in demand. Her eyes were sunk in their sockets and she looked as if she had spent too many nights awake singing, also as if she had been drinking too much tuak. She had a staring though not unpleasant expression, was devoted to her religious exercises, and possessed an interesting personality.

A majority of the women was disinclined to face the

UPPER KATINGANS PASSING THE RAPIDS OF BUNTUT MANGKIKIT

From a kinematograph film

UPPER KATINGAN WOMEN DANCING. BUNTUT MANGKIKIT

From a kinematograph film

UPPER KATINGAN FAMILY, AT BUNTUT MANGKIKIT
An unusual couple, the kapala and his wife, who was a great medicine woman

camera, one of them explaining that she was not ashamed but was afraid. However, an example in acquiescence was set by the blian and her family. She wore for the occasion an ancient Katingan bodice fitting snugly around the body, with tight sleeves, the material showing foreign influence but not the style of making. Another woman was dressed in the same way, and a big gold plate hung over the upper part of the chest, as is the prevailing mode among women and children. Gold is said to be found in the ground and the Katingans themselves make it into ornaments. Many of the men wore chavats.

Of the men that were measured, one was sombre brown, darker than the rest, and three harelips were observed. A man may have from one to three wives, who sometimes fight, but all ends well. In each family there are at least two children, and often as many as seven, while one woman had borne eleven, of whom only four survived. The feminine fashion in hair-dressing is the same as that followed by the Duhoi, which looks well, the hair folded over on each side with some locks tied over the middle. I saw here two implements called duhong, knives shaped like broad spear points, relics of ancient times, with which the owners would not part. The Katingans are probably the friendliest and best tempered Dayaks I met. The children are tender hearted: when the kapala's nude little son, about two and a half years old, approached my film box his father spoke harshly to him; the child immediately began to cry bitterly and his mother, the great blian, soothed and affectionately kissed him until he became calm.

The obliging kapala, in order to do his bit to induce the people to dance, offered to present one pig if I would give rice and salt. The dancing, which was performed around a blanga on a mat spread on the ground, was similar in character to what may be seen elsewhere in Borneo. Four men and four women performed one dance. In another only women took part, and they moved one behind another in a circle with unusually quick, short steps, signifying that good antohs had taken possession of them. The principal blian later sat down on a mat and sang; three women sitting near accompanied her by beating small oblong drums. They all became enthusiastic, for music attracts good antohs. In the Katingan language the word lauk means creature; an additional word, earth, water, or air, as the case may be, signifying whether an animal, a bird, or a fish is meant.

Having accomplished in a short time as much as could be expected, we returned to Kuala Samba, and from there, in the first week of January, started southward in our big prahu. The river was very low, and after half an hour we were compelled to take on board two Bakompai men as pilots among the sand banks. At Bali the coffin was found to be ready and was taken on board. It had been well-made, but the colours were mostly, if not all, obtained from the trader and came off easily, which was somewhat disappointing. It seemed smaller than the original, though the makers insisted that it was quite similar and challenged me to go and see the one they had copied, which was in the vicinity, behind the kampong.

AN UPPER KATINGAN, OF BUNT JT MANGKIKIT. FRONT, SIDE, AND BACK VIEWS

UPPER KATINGAN WOMEN AT BUNTUT MANGKIKIT, FRONT AND SIDE VIEWS

On one of them the scaly skin disease is distinctly seen

Here I saw a new and somewhat striking arrangement for the disposition of the dead. A small white house contained several coffins guarded by seven kapatongs of medium size, which stood in a row outside, with the lower part of their legs and bodies wrapped in mats. The skull of a water-buffalo and many pigs' jaws hung near by. Two tall memorial staffs, called pantars, had been erected, but instead of the wooden image of the great hornbill which usually adorns the top, the Dutch flag presented itself to view. Appearing beautiful to the Dayaks it had been substituted for the bird. The all-important second funeral having been celebrated, the dead occupied their final resting place.

We spent the night at a large kampong where there was a fine, straightforward kapala who appeared at a disadvantage only when, with intent to please me, he wore clothes, but from whom I gained valuable information. He also had a sense of humour, and next day when our coffin was carried ashore, in order that I might be enlightened in regard to the significance of its decorations, he laughed heartily and exclaimed in astonishment at the sight. With the exception of the upper part of the back, few parts of his body were left uncovered with tatu marks. Over and below each knee he had extra designs to protect him from disease, he said, each of which represented a fish of ancient times.

At our next and last stopping-place the small pasang grahan, on very tall poles, was in poor condition and the roof was full of holes, but the kapala, an uncommonly satisfactory man—there was no Malay about him—saw to it that rough palm-leaf mats were placed above the ceiling to protect against possible rain, and two large rattan mats were spread on the shaky floor, so we had a good camping-place. There was an unusually pretty view of the majestic river from up there, including a wide bend just below. Experience modifies one's requirements, and I felt content as I took my bath at the outer corner of the shed, high above the still water on which the moon shone placidly.

SAMPLES OF DAYAK TATUING

The figure of a man represents a Lower Katingan, particularly a kapala at Tewang Rongkang, the only one I saw with tatu marks on the knees. These depict a fish of ancient times. On each thigh is the representation of a dog or possibly the nagah with a dog's head.

The central tatu design represents a tree, the trunk of which rises from the navel; adjoining it above are two great oval designs stretching across the chest and depicting the wings of a fowl. The tree which is called garing, is a fabulous one that cannot be killed. This same pattern may be observed on the mats of the Kayans.

Down the arms and over the shoulders are similar designs representing leaves of the areca palm.

The border around the wrist is a representation of a bird called susulit. The cross on the hand represents the beak of this bird; the starlike figure is the eye of the hornbill.

The globular tatu mark on the calf of the leg (h) is peculiar to Katingans, Ot-Danums, and other tribes. The design below, representing a certain fruit, was seen on a Katingan.

The seven tatu marks to the right (a, b, c, d, e, f, g) represent the durian in various phases. The upper (a) to the left is a ripe durian, a design often observed in the tribes, one on each shoulder of a man. The next three (b, c, d) are young fruit, often seen one above each nipple. The next figure (e), usually observed on the upper arm (in front) represents 14 durians.

Above the nails of the tatued hand of a Penihing woman (f) are seen similar triangular marks, while across it runs a border representing the protuberances of the fruit. The latter designs are also found on the foot (g) of the same individual. The cross lines over fingers and toes represent banana leaves.

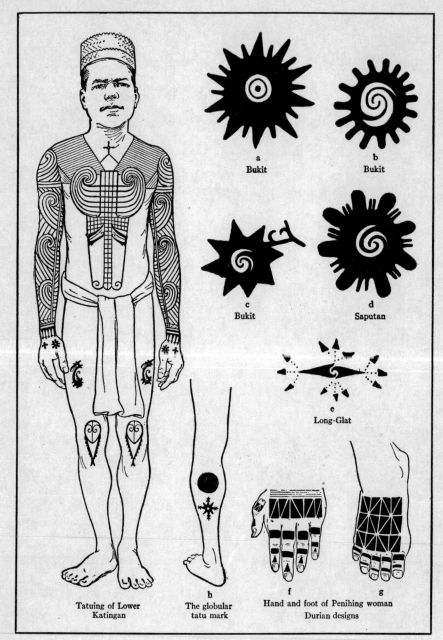

a Bukit	**b** Bukit
c Bukit	**d** Saputan

e
Long-Glat

Tatuing of Lower
Katingan

h
The globular
tatu mark

f   **g**
Hand and foot of Penihing woman
Durian designs

SAMPLES OF DAYAK TATUING

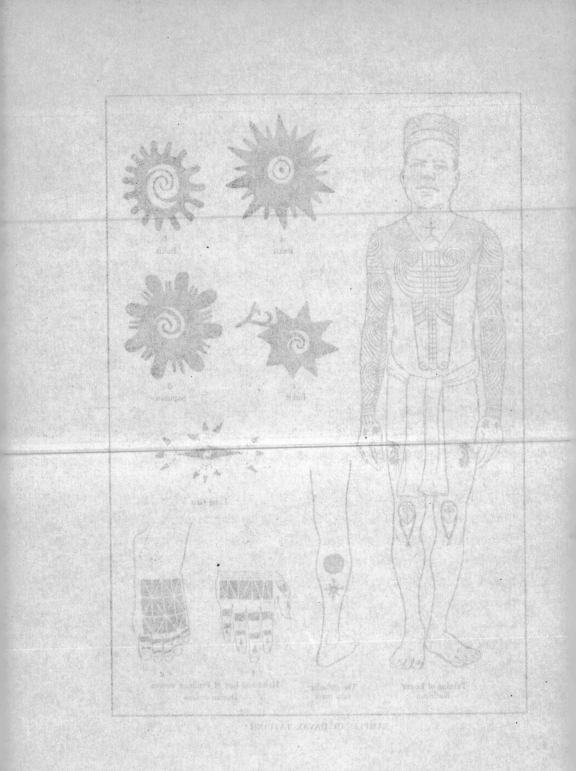

CHAPTER XXXIII

KASUNGAN—THE WEALTH OF THE DAYAKS—ANIMISM—
GUARDIANS OF THE DEAD—HUGE SERPENTS—CROCO-
DILES—GOVERNMENT OF DAYS GONE BY—KATINGAN
CUSTOMS AND BELIEFS

NEXT day we arrived at Kasungan, where we were offered quarters in a large room in the "onder's" house. There was no news of our steamer, the *Selatan,* and I remained about a week. The "onder," a Kahayan who had been here twenty-five years, had the intelligence and reliability that seems characteristic of the Dayaks of the Kahayan and Kapuas Rivers, and, as a matter of course, possessed extensive knowledge of the Katingan. He had lately been converted to Christianity. The kampong was quite large, and although it has been subject to the influence of Malay traders a long time and quite recently to that of a missionary, still the natives offered considerable of interest. It is only eight years since the communal house obtained. Before some of the houses stand grotesque kapatongs, and the majority of the population lives in the atmosphere of the long ago. I was still able to buy ethnological articles and implements which are becoming increasingly difficult to secure.

On entering a house the salutation is, *Akko domo* (I (akko) arrive). To this is answered, *Munduk* (Sit down). On leaving the visitor says, *Akko buhao* (I am going). To which is responded, Come again. On my way to visit

349

a prominent Katingan I passed beneath a few cocoanut trees growing in front of the house, as is the custom, while a gentle breeze played with the stately leaves. "Better get away from there," my native guide suddenly said; "a cocoanut may fall," and we had scarcely arrived inside the house before one fell to the ground with a resounding thump half a metre from where I had been standing. Eighteen years previously a Katingan had been killed in this way as he descended the ladder. Eleven years later another was carrying his child on his back when a cocoanut of small size hit and killed the little one.

The man whose house I visited was rich, according to Dayak standard, not in money, but in certain wares that to him are of equal or greater value. Besides thirty gongs, rows of fine old valuable jars stood along the walls of his room. There are several varieties of these blangas, some of which are many hundred years old and come from China or Siam. This man possessed five of the expensive kind, estimated by the "onder" at a value of six thousand florins each. He consented to have one of the ordinary kind, called gutshi, taken outside to be photographed; to remove the real blanga, he said, would necessitate the sacrifice of a fowl. To the casual observer no great difference between them is apparent, their worth being enhanced by age. In 1880 Controleur Michielsen saw thirty blangas in one house on the Upper Katingan, among them several that in his estimation were priceless. Over them hung forty gongs, of which the biggest, unquestionably, had a diameter of one metre. Without exaggeration it represented, he says,

WOMEN BEATING SMALL DRUMS AND SINGING. BUNTUT MANGKIKIT

Upper Katingans share the usual belief of the Dayaks that good spirits are attracted by music

STAFFS, CALLED PANTARS, ERECTED IN MEMORIAM OF
THE DEAD, AT A KAMPONG BELOW KUALA SAMBA

PROTECTING AGAINST EVIL SPIRITS. KASUNGAN
The carved representation of a tiger cat, holding a human head, serves
as a warning to evil spirits

a value of f. 15,000, and he was informed that the most valuable blangas were buried in the wilds at places known only to the owner. No European had been there since Schwaner, over thirty years previously, passed the river.

In front of another house was a group of very old-looking stones which are considered to be alive, though such is not the belief with reference to all stones, information in that regard being derived from dreams. Those on view here are regarded as slaves (or soldiers) of a raja, who is represented by a small kapatong which presides in a diminutive, half-tumbled-down house, and who is possessed by a good antoh that may appear in human shape at night. When the people of the kampong need rice or have any other wish, a fowl or pig is killed; the blood is smeared on the raja and on the slaves, and some of the meat is deposited in a jar standing next to him. When advised of what is wanted the raja gives the slaves orders to see that the people are supplied.

At each side of the base of a ladder, a little further on, stood a post with a carving of a tiger-cat grasping a human head and guarding the entrance. They are a protection to the owner of the house against evil antohs; it is as if they were saying: "Keep away, antoh! You see I slew a man, so you know what will happen to you!"

The bones of dead persons were kept at the back of at least one dwelling, inside the appropriate small house provided for the purpose, and some curious kapatongs of large size were to be seen, some of which had guarded the dead for more than a hundred years. One has the head of a good antoh, showing big corner teeth and out-hanging tongue, as he watches that no bad antohs come to injure the dead man's soul.

A woman carrying a betel box is believed to watch well because when chewing betel one does not sleep; but in her case there must always be a male kapatong near by, for a woman alone is not sufficient protection. Betel makes the mouth and lips beautiful in the estimation of the natives, therefore many kapatongs are seen with betel box in hand.

A very extraordinary guardian of the dead is a loving pair, the man's arm placed affectionately over the shoulder of his companion. Lovers do not sleep, hence they are good at watching, reasons the Dayak.

In these regions I gathered some information about the huge serpent of which one hears occasionally in Borneo, called sahua by the Malays, and which, according to accounts, may attain a length of seven or eight metres. It is able to remain long under water, moves slowly on land, and can climb trees. Deer and pigs are its usual food, but at times it attacks and eats natives. A few years previously this python devoured a Katingan, and as it remains at the same place for some time after a meal, two days later it was found and killed. These Dayaks kill it with knives, spears being ineffectual, and the meat is eaten. A very large lizard is also said to be a man-eater.

Crocodiles are numerous here, and at low water have been responsible for the disappearance of many Katingans. They are considered good antohs, but if one of the monsters devours a man arrangements are made to kill it, though otherwise the natives prefer not to do so and do not eat it. For the purpose of capture they use a piece of strong wood, about three centimetres thick, pointed at each end. A line of fibre a metre long is tied to the middle, and about half a metre above the surface of the water an ill-smelling monkey or dog is suspended from it as bait. When swallowed by the crocodile the stick usually becomes wedged in the mouth between the upper and lower jaws and he is hauled ashore.

A few years before my visit the brother of the kapala was eaten by a crocodile as he and two other Katingans were fishing with a casting-net. While sitting in the prahu he was attacked by the animal and dragged below the surface of the water. The entire kampong was incensed and believed that a bad antoh had ordered the crocodile to commit the evil deed. A babi was immediately killed and the blood sacrificed to induce a good antoh to come and help them; they also danced for the same purpose, while some of them prepared the material with which to catch the reptile. They have been fishing for crocodiles ever since, for their religion prohibits quitting until the bait is taken either by the large fish, tapa, or by the python, called sahua. When either of these huge animals swallows the bait, that event is regarded as a sign from a good antoh to the effect that their task is finished. Many years may elapse before the message comes and the kapala, who had caught fifty, must still continue, for twenty years if necessary, until the sign appears.

When preparing to kill crocodiles the magic use of rice is as essential as when the lives of men are to be taken, proceedings in both cases being identical. If a Katingan wants to get a head he must pay the blian to conjure with rice—a cupful is enough—and to dance. To have this done costs one or two florins. During incantations and dancing the blian throws the rice in the direction of the country where the man wants to operate. By the act of throwing the rice an antoh is called to assist and he causes the intended victim to become stupid and forgetful, therefore easily killed. From two to seven days later a start is made on the expedition, and when the head is cut the rice is sure to be found inside.

In earlier days the kampongs were ruled by hereditary rajas called bakas, who held their people in firm subjection, and they are reported to have fought much among themselves. According to the "onder" of the kampong, it was not an unusual occurrence to murder a rich man and take his goods as well as his head, and as murder could not be compensated with money, his relatives having to avenge the deed, a vendetta ensued which might last five or six years. A custom which required a debtor to become the slave of his creditor, even in the case of brothers, has been abolished.

Formerly when an enemy approached a curious message was sent from kampong to kampong. To the top of a spear was tied a tail feather of the rhinoceros hornbill, symbolising rapid movement, and also a woman's skirt of fibre with a bunch of odoriferous leaves attached. Women used to fasten these to the skirt in addition to

A WEALTHY KATINGAN, AT KASUNGAN

The riches of a Dayak are not measured in cash but in the possession of ancient jars and beads

SACRIFICE OF EGGS TO THE GOOD SPIRITS. LONG PAHANGEI, MAHAKAM RIVER
This kind of sacrifice is in general use among the Dayaks visited

A LOVING PAIR GUARDING THE DEAD. KASUNGAN

those placed in the hair. This meant an urgent order for people to gather quickly for the fight, and in the event of failure to obey the call promptly the leaves and skirt signified unworthiness to wear masculine attire.

Two methods of fire-making were in use here, by drilling or by friction with a rope made of fibre or rattan across a block of wood. The Katingan does not know the art of doing inlaid work on the blade of the parang, in which Kenyahs and Kayans excel, and he makes no earthen ware. Hair that has been cut from the head must be placed in a tree. Their sacred number is seven, as is that of the Ot-Danum, Kapuas, and Kahayan. As usual with Dayaks, all members of the family eat at the same time as the men. Sons and daughters inherit equally, while brothers and sisters receive nothing unless the deceased was childless.

The father of a young man must arrange the payment for the bride, and probably receives remuneration himself for the service rendered. The son-in-law remains in the house of his father-in-law a year or more and assists him. A raja was privileged to have five or six wives.

During the period of pregnancy both wife and husband are subject to the following restrictions:

1. They must not split firewood, otherwise harelip will result, or a child with double thumbs.

2. The arms or legs must not be cut off from any animal caught, else the child will have stumps of arms or legs.

3. When fish has been caught the couple must not open the head themselves; if they do the child will be born without ears.

4. The husband must not make fish hooks, or the child will be born doubled up in a wrong position, perhaps causing the mother's death.

5. Neither of them may stretch up either arm to take food from the hanging trays of bamboo, called toyang. Should they do so the child will come into the world arm first, or probably not be born.

6. They must not nail up boxes or anything else (nails were formerly of wood), nor tie up anything,—for instance, a rattan for drying clothes,—nor lock a trunk, else the child will not be born and the mother will die.

7. In case of feeling hot, if he or she should take off their upper garments they must not be tied round the neck, or the child will be born dead, with the navel cord around its neck.

8. The work of tying split bamboo sticks into loose mats, for instance such as are used in the bottom of the prahu, must not be done, or the child will be born with two and two or all four fingers grown together.

9. They must not put the cork in a bottle or place the cover on a bamboo basket containing rice in order to close it for a considerable time, as in that case the child will be born blind in one or both eyes, or with one ear, one nostril, or the rectum closed, but the cover may be put back on a basket from which rice is taken for daily use.

10. For five months the work of putting a handle on a parang and fastening it with damar must not be done else both mother and child would die.

The name given the child when the umbilical cord is

cut remains unchanged. Among names in vogue here for men are Bugis (black), Spear, Axe, Duhong (ancient knife), etc., Tingang and other names of birds, or names taken from animals, fish, trees, and fruit; many are called Peti, the Malay name for a steel trunk sold by traders. A person must not give his own name nor call by the name of his father, mother, father-in-law, mother-in-law, grandfather or grandmother, whether they are alive or dead. If one of these names is given there will be no luck, for instance, in fishing or hunting.

There are many sorts of páli (sins) but all may be paid for in kind or by sacrifice. One of the most serious is that of a widow who marries before the second funeral of her husband has been solemnised. Although the rule does not apply to husband and wife, a man is forbidden to touch a woman's dress and vice versa, and transgression must be made good by sacrifice of a fowl or even a pig. In case a chavat or other article of clothing belonging to a man has been hung to dry after washing, and a woman other than his wife wishes to take the garment from the rattan line, she must use a stick for the purpose.

Every big tree is believed to have an antoh in possession of it, some being well disposed, others of evil disposition. When a man is killed by falling from a tree, members of his family come and proceed to hit it with darts blown from the sumpitan, cut it with parangs, spear it, and as final punishment it is felled. Many people gather, angry with the tree antoh, and a feast is made for the purpose of calling a good spirit to drive away or kill the bad one.

When a large tree falls no work is done for seven days. House building must cease and sacrificial offerings of pork and tuak are made to a good antoh to induce him to deal with the evil one that caused the mishap.

Travellers who encounter omen birds, or hear the cry of a rusa at noon, or similar omens, camp for three days and then proceed to the nearest kampong to buy fowl, a pig, and eggs, in order to sacrifice not only to the bird or animal that gave the omen, but also to the good antoh which sent it. Seven days afterward the journey is continued.

When a plandok (mouse-deer) appears underneath a house the owner is sure to die unless proper remedies are employed. If people succeed in catching the animal it is not killed, but smeared all over with cocoanut oil. Then they kill a dog, take its blood, which is mixed with rice and thrown to the plandok; also the blood of a fowl, with the same addition, is offered. The plandok's liao is given this to eat in order that he may not cause the occupant of the house to die; the animal is then carried into the utan, about an hour's walk, and set free. Three days afterward they sacrifice a pig, the blood of which, with the usual admixture, is given to the bad antoh who sent the plandok, with entreaties not to kill the man. For seven days the head of the house stays in the kampong, being free to bathe in the river and walk about, but he must not go outside the settlement.

The red monkey is an attendant of a bad antoh, and if he enters a house or comes on the roof or underneath the house it is considered very unfortunate. There is no remedy and the owner must move elsewhere; the house is demolished, the wooden material carried away and erected in another kampong. Should he remain at the same place there would be much strife between him and his neighbours. If a wah-wah climbs on a roof the house will burn down. There is no remedy for this either; the incumbent leaves and makes a new home.

On the other hand, should a scaly ant-eater enter a room it is a joyful event, indicating that the owner will become rich. The animal is caught, blood from a fowl is smeared over him, and he is carried back to the utan.

If it should so happen that a red-backed lizard, a timid animal rather common about kampongs, enters a house it also brings good luck. A good antoh gave it the order to come, and it means much paddi, a gutshi, and other good things. Three fowls must be sacrificed and the people also dance.

CHAPTER XXXIV

FUNERAL CUSTOMS OF THE KATINGANS—DEPARTURE FROM
KASUNGAN—AN ATTEMPTED VISIT TO SEMBULO—IN-
DIFFERENT MALAYS—A STRANGE DISEASE—THE BE-
LIEF IN TAILED PEOPLE—THE LEGEND OF THE ANCES-
TOR OF TAILED MEN

WHEN a liao departs through the top of the head and
death occurs, gongs are beaten for twenty-four hours.
Five or six men set to work to make a beautiful coffin
similar to the one already described; this is often finished
in a day and the corpse, having been washed, is immediately placed within it. For a man a new chavat of
wood fibre is adjusted around the loins, without other
vestments. Another day is consumed in the work of
decorating the coffin, which is done by men, while women
weave diminutive mats, which are left less than half
finished and are laid on top of the casket. For three
days and as many nights the remains are kept in the
house, and, if a man, his duhong (ancient knife), parang,
knife, spear, sumpitan, betel box, tobacco container, and
much food are placed nearby.

After these matters have received attention, food is
eaten by those present. Fires are kept burning within
the house and also outside, and after each meal the people strike one another's legs with firebrands in order to
forget their grief. Members of the family, who begin to
wail immediately after his death, continue to do so con-

stantly for seven days, and they wear no red garments until after the tiwah feast which constitutes his second funeral. The coffin is buried in the ground or placed on a crude platform, and, when this work is finished, thorough ablution in water containing leaves which possess qualities especially adapted to this purpose is the rule for everybody concerned. This is done to the end that no odour of the dead shall linger, thus exposing the living to danger from the bad antoh that is responsible for the unfortunate event which necessitated their recent activities. Later, all partake of tuak, including the children.

After this preliminary disposal of the body the family begins to plan for the second and final funeral, which is considered a compensation to the departed soul for the property he left behind. Caution demands that they be very punctilious about this, for the ghost, though believed to be far above this plane, is thought to be resentful, with power to cause misfortunes of various kinds and therefore is feared. Until recently, when a man of means died, a slave had to be killed and his head placed on top of the coffin. When time for the second funeral, the tiwah, came round another slave was killed and his head hung near by. They are his attendants in the next life, but many more and elaborate arrangements are necessary to satisfy the demands of the liao, and they must be fully complied with on the celebration of the tiwah, the most elaborate of all feasts in Borneo.

When the deceased is well-to-do this observance may follow immediately, but usually years go by and many liaoes are served at the same time. On the great occasion the coffin is put on a big fire for a couple of hours until the flesh has been burned from the bones, which are then collected in a small box and placed in a house of limited proportions especially constructed for this purpose and called sandung.   It is made of ironwood, and in these regions the people have a preference for placing it high above the ground, but it may also be put underground in a subterranean chamber also made of ironwood, which may take five or six months to construct and which is large enough to accommodate a family.   The feast lasts one week, during which food and tuak are provided. Every night the women dance inside the house, around a tree composed of many bamboo stalks placed together so as to form a large trunk.   As elsewhere mentioned, (p. 142), the dancing, which is similar to that which follows the harvest, is for the benefit of the ghost and is distinct from the usual performance.

As soon as the tiwah feast has been decided upon the people start simultaneously to perfect the various arrangements, some looking for a water-buffalo or two, others beginning to make the several contrivances which the occasion demands.   Many men are thus occupied for several months.   There are experts in the required handiwork, though a skilful man may be capable of performing all the various tasks.   In earlier days the different memorials and the box containing the bones were placed in front of the house of the deceased, but of late years government officials have made some changes in this arrangement.   When preparing for a tiwah feast it was the custom to close the river for perhaps three

PANYANGGARAN, AT BALI, KATINGAN RIVER

PANYANGGARAN, AT KASUNGAN, KATINGAN RIVER

This important device, to which the sacrificial animal is t ed at the second funeral of a man, exhibits, at the top, the rules for the widow

TAMOANS, FROM BANGKAL, LAKE SEMBULO, FRONT AND SIDE VIEWS

months by suspending a rattan rope on which were hung many spears of wood, tail feathers of the great hornbill, and leaves of certain trees. After a head had been secured the impediment was removed, but the government has forbidden the temporary obstruction.

A most important matter is the construction of the device to which the water-buffalo, formerly the slave, is tied when sacrificed. In its make-up it expresses symbolically the rules of behaviour for the widow until after the feast has been celebrated. Its name is panyanggaran, an obscure word which probably may be derived from sangar, which means to kill; the place of killing.

The foundation is a large post, usually of ironwood, firmly planted in the ground; its top is pointed and a little below, on either side, is attached horizontally a piece of dressed wood like two arms. Further below a number of sticks are affixed to each side, pointing obliquely upward, and all on a plane with the arms above. These sticks, usually three on each side but sometimes more, are considered as spears, and the top of each is finished with a rosette representing four spear-points, called kalapiting. The post itself is also regarded as a spear and is called *balu* (widow), while the sticks are named *pampang-balu* (widow rules). It seems possible that the post also represents the woman, head, arms, and body being recognisable. However that may be, the attached sticks are regarded as so many rules and reminders for the widow. In Kasungan I saw in one case eight sticks, in another only four. The rules may thus vary or be applicable to different cases, though some are fundamental.

Assuming that the requirements are six in number, according to my informant, the following should be observed by the widow: (1) To make the tiwah feast; (2) to refrain from remarriage until the feast has been celebrated; (3) to abstain from sexual intercourse; (4) to remain in the same place until after the feast; (5) to ask permission from the family of the deceased if she wants to leave the kampong temporarily; (6) to wear no red garments until the feast has been completed. Should any of these injunctions be disregarded a gutshi, the value of which may be twenty florins, must be paid to his relatives. If the widow desires to marry earlier than the tiwah feast she is required to pay the entire cost of the celebration, and sometimes an additional amount.

A simpler device than the panyanggaran is also used, serving a similar purpose and called sapundo. It consists of an upright post carved to represent the face of a good antoh, with tongue hanging out. To this pillar is tied a water-buffalo (as substitute for the slave formerly employed), a cow, or pig. As the sapundo is much easier to make it is used by the orang kampong or poor people. For a rich man who has gone hence both contrivances may be erected.

Another matter demanding attention is the erection of a tall, rather slender pole of ironwood, called pantar. A gong or gutshi strung near the top signifies that the deceased was a person of wealth and prominence, while a wooden image of the rhinoceros hornbill occupies a lofty position on the pinnacle. On account of its ability to discern objects at a great distance, this bird is regarded as a good watchman to guard the sacrifice, whether it be a water-buffalo or other animal. The pantar itself simply means "in memoriam," as if enjoining: "Don't forget this man!" These primitive monuments sometimes last over a hundred years, and more than one may be raised for the same man. Should it prove impossible to secure a water-buffalo, an ordinary cow may serve as sacrifice. The family thereby presents the animal's liao (soul) to the liao of the deceased, and the blian by dancing and sacrifice calls the latter to come and eat. Not only this, but the liao of every animal, bird, and fish which the family eats from the time of his death until the tiwah feast is given to him. Account is kept by incised cross-cuts on certain posts, notifying him of the number. I was told that when a raja died similar marks of account were made on a slave. The jaws of pigs or other animals, hanging by scores in the houses, together with heads of fish and legs of birds, are similar accounts for the same purpose, and all close with the tiwah feast.

A kapatong must be made, or, if the deceased were rich, perhaps two or three, which are inaugurated by the blian in the usual way, to be the ghost's attendants and guardians. The remaining duties to be performed are the making of a box or coffin for the bones to rest in, and the house in which it is to be deposited, either above or under the ground as may be decided. These tasks accomplished, no further responsibility devolves upon the widow or other members of the family.

On my return journey I stopped a few hours at a kampong in the vicinity to see some stones that, according to Katingan belief, are alive and multiplying. As my visit was expected, a fowl had just been sacrificed to these guardians of the kampong, and a fire made from bark was burning near by to keep the stones comfortable, so they would not be angry at being photographed. There were two roundish specimens, almost honeycombed with small cavities, one of them, scarcely twenty-five centimetres high, being regarded as masculine and the other, smaller and covered with green moss, was supposed to be of feminine gender. Originally, as the story goes, only these two were there, but later six "children" appeared, as evidenced by six smaller stones lying close to the "parents." The domain held sacred to this interesting family was bounded by four pieces of wood, each about a metre in length. Over all was extended a small square piece of red cloth supported on four upright sticks, which had been placed there two weeks before on behalf of a sick man whose recovery was attributed to this act of veneration. In front of the small enclosure lay four stones of inconsiderable size, lying in two pairs and supposed to be attendants; in the rear was a small house, reputed to be over three hundred years old, its purpose being to protect the stones, where offerings of food, with skulls of deer and pigs, were deposited.

Next day we met the *Selatan* on its way up the river, brought our luggage on board, and continued our journey. We had a disagreeable night before arriving at Bandjermasin; in fact, it is risky to travel south of Borneo in a steam-launch in January. As the wind was strong and the waves were too high for us to proceed, anchor was thrown and we were tossed about, the lamps went out, and, according to the captain, the boat nearly turned over. Mr. Loing, prostrate with seasickness, saved himself from being thrown overboard by grasping the rail.

After packing my collections I again set out for Sampit with the intention of revisiting Sembulo by another route, proceeding by prahu up the Kuala Sampit as far as possible, and then marching overland to the lake. The controleur was absent, but his native clerk and the kapala together got me the prahus and the men, such as the place afforded. As usual, the Malay coolies were late in arriving and began making many difficulties about various things. To cheer them I gave each f. 1.50 in advance, which made them all happy, and in buoyant, talkative spirits they immediately went off to buy rice, dried fish, tobacco, cigarettes, and other things. All was well, and at ten o'clock in the morning we finally started, with a native policeman in attendance.

An hour later the coolies wanted to cook rice. It did not take long to discover that they were not very useful, though the clerk had done his best. Two brothers were intolerably lazy, continually resting the paddles, lighting cigarettes, washing their faces, etc., the elder, after the full meal they had eaten, actually falling asleep at times. The interest of the men centred in eating and early camping, and we made slow progress, detained besides by a thunder-storm, as it was impossible to make headway against the strong wind. The man at the helm of the small prahu was intelligent, and from him I finally obtained information about a place to stop for the night.

At six o'clock we arrived at the mouth of the Kuala Sampit, where we found it difficult to effect a landing on account of the dilapidated condition of the landing-float. Some distance from the water stood a lonely house, in genuine Malay style, with high-gabled roof. The stairs afforded precarious access, a condition which may have been regarded as a protection, but more likely it was due to laziness and want of care. However that may have been, the interior was surprisingly substantial, with an excellent floor like that in a ball-room. I slept in a detached ramshackle room used as a kitchen, comfortable because of being open to the air.

In the morning the Malays were again too late. I was ready for a start at six o'clock, but about that time they began to cook. The small river, perhaps twenty metres wide, is deep enough to have allowed a steam-launch of the *Selatan's* dimensions to go as far as the kampong Rongkang, our first destination, and there is little current. At five o'clock we had to stop to give the men opportunity to prepare their rice, and in the evening we arrived at Rongkang. The gongs were being beaten lustily in the darkness; we thought it must be on account of a death, which proved to be the case, a woman having died some days before. The house which was placed at my disposal was more nearly air-tight than usual.

The kapala said it was difficult to get men, but he would do his best. A strange epidemic had lately appeared, and some deaths had occurred in the kampongs of this region. In the room I occupied a woman had recently recovered from an attack of a week's duration. The disease, which probably is a variety of cholera, was described to me as being a severe diarrhœa accompanied by vomiting, paralysis, and fever, the crisis occurring in three to five days. The disorder appears to rise from the feet, and if it settles between the liver and heart may prove fatal in half a day. As I learned later, this illness, which the Malays call men-tjo-tjok, is usually present in the inland region of the Sampit River, and is also found on the upper parts of the Kahayan and Pembuang Rivers.

People in this neighbourhood were lappar (hungry), having no rice, and the men were absent in the utan looking for rattan, white damar, and rubber, which they exchange for rice from Chinese traders. Under such circumstances, chiefly women and children are left in the kampongs. Of nearly thirty men needed for my overland trip, only three could be mustered here. One Dayak who was perfectly well in the evening came next morning to consult me about the prevalent illness which he had contracted during the night. The only available course was to return to Sampit.

The name of the Dayaks here and on Lake Sembulo is Tamoan (or Samoan), with intermixture of Katingans, who are said to understand each other's language. Most of these friendly natives had fair-sized beards, some only mustaches. The elder men complainingly said that the younger ones no longer want to tatu nor cut the front teeth.   No haste was apparent about making the coffin for the woman who had been dead four days; although not yet commenced they said it would be completed that day.

The left bank of the river is much higher than the right, which is flooded, therefore the utan on that side presents a very different appearance, with large, fine-looking trees and no dense underbrush.   All was fresh and calm after the rain which prevails at this season (February).   There were showers during the afternoon, at times heavy, and the Malays were much opposed to getting wet, wanting to stop paddling, notwithstanding the fact that the entire prahu was covered with an atap. As we approached the mouth of the river, where I intended to camp for the night, I noticed a prahu halting at the rough landing place of a ladang, and as we passed it the rain poured down.   When the single person who was paddling arose to adjust the scanty wet clothing I perceived that it was a woman, and looking back I discovered her husband snugly at ease under a palm-leaf mat raised as a cover.   He was then just rising to walk home.   That is the way the men of Islam treat their women.   Even one of the Malay paddlers saw the humour of the situation and laughed.

At Rongkang I was told the legend of the dog that in ancient times had come from the inland of Borneo to Sembulo, where it became progenitor of the tailed people. In various parts of Borneo I heard about natives with short tails, and there are to-day otherwise reliable Dayaks, Malays, and even Chinese, who insist that they

have seen them.   Especially in regard to their presence
at the lake of Sembulo, at the kampong of the same name,
the consensus of opinion is strong.   That place is the
classical ground for the rumour of tailed men, and I
thought it worth while, before leaving Borneo, to make
another attempt later to reach Sembulo and investigate
the reasons for the prevalent belief in tailed humans in
that locality.   The most complete legend on this subject
I obtained from a prominent ex-district kapala, Kiai
Laman, a Kahayan Dayak converted to Islam.   He has
travelled much in certain sections of Borneo, is interested
in folklore matters, and told his stories without apparent
errors or contradictions.   The tale here rendered is from
the Ot-Danums on the Upper Kahayan River.

A male dog called Bélang started out to hunt for game
—pig, deer, plandok.   The kampong heard him bark
in the manner common to dogs when on the trail of an
animal, and then the baying ceased.   The owner watched
for the animal to return, but for half a year there was no
news of him.   In the meantime the dog had gone to
Sembulo, making the trip in fifteen days.   He appeared
there in the shape of a man, took part in the work of the
kampong, and married.   His wife bore a child who had a
tail, not long, about ten centimetres.   "I do not like to
tell a lie," said my raconteur.   "What the sex was I
do not know, but people say it was a male infant.   She
had another child, a female, also with a tail."

In the ladang the woman thought the crying of her
children sounded very strange.   "It is not like that of
other infants," she said.   "Other people have no tails

and you have; you look like the children of a dog."
Their father replied: "In truth I am a dog," and immediately he resumed his natural form, ran away, and after
an interval arrived in the Upper Kahayan, where his
owner welcomed him, and the dog lived to old age and
died.

In due time the two children married and had large
families, all of whom had tails, but since the Malays
came and married Sembulo women the tails have become shorter and shorter. At present most of the people have none, and those that remain are not often seen
because clothes are now worn; however, many travellers
to Sembulo have beheld them.

The rendering from Rongkal is similar, with this difference: The man from Upper Kahayan followed his
dog—which at sight of his master resumed canine form—
and killed it. According to a Malay version, a raja of
Bandjermasin was much disliked and the people made
him leave the country. He took a female dog with him
in the prahu and went to Sembulo, where he had children
all of whom had tails.

CHAPTER XXXV

A VISIT TO KUALA KAPUAS—A BREED OF STUMP-TAILED
DOGS—THE SHORT-TAILED CATS OF BORNEO—A SEC-
OND EXPEDITION TO LAKE SEMBULO—NATIVES UNDIS-
MAYED BY BERI-BERI—THE TAMOANS—THE PRACTICE
OF INCISION

THE second trip to Sembulo had to be postponed
until the return of the controleur of Sampit from an
extended tour, when the steam-launch *Selatan* would
again be placed at my service. During the weeks of
waiting I made a trip to Kuala Kapuas, northwest of
Bandjermasin. The Kapuas River is broad here, I
should say at least 600 metres; if there is any wind one
cannot cross because the prahus are all made of ironwood and sink easily, owing to the fact that they are
heavy and do not accommodate themselves to the waves.
A German missionary and family had been here ten
years. The children looked a little pale but strong, and
had never had malaria nor children's diseases.

I soon became convinced that there was little here for
me to learn. The Dayaks have been too long exposed
to Malay and European influences, though still able to
make splendid mats, for which this place is well known.
Malay ascendancy is strong on the lower courses of the
two great rivers that meet here, on the Kapuas as far
as Djangkang, on the Kahayan as far as Pahandut. I
carried away mud for future zoological examination from
the bottom of a pool, ten minutes walk from the shore.

There are always small fish in it, and three or four times a year it is flooded. In dry seasons, although not every year, the water of the sea reaches as far as Mandumei.

In Bandjermasin my attention was drawn to an interesting breed of stump-tailed dogs which belonged to Mr. B. Brouers. The mother is a white terrier which has but half a tail, as if cut off. When she had pups, two had stump tails, two had long ones, and one had none; her sister has no tail. Though the fathers are the ordinary yellowish Dayak dogs with long tails, the breed apparently has taken nothing or next to nothing from them. They are all white, sometimes with hardly noticeable spots of yellow.

Nobody who has travelled in Borneo can have failed to notice the great number of short-tailed cats. In Bandjermasin those with long tails are very rare, and among Malays and Dayaks I do not remember ever having seen them. They are either stub-tailed or they have a ball at the end of a tail that is usually twisted and exceptionally short. These cats are small and extremely tame, and can hardly be pushed away with a kick, because they have always been used to having their own way in the house. They are more resourceful and enterprising than the ordinary domestic cat, using their claws to an almost incredible extent in climbing down perpendicular wooden walls, or in running under the roof on rafters chasing mice. I have twice photographed such cats, a liberty which they resented by striking viciously at the man who held them and growling all the time. Their accustomed food is rice and dried fish.

The steamship *Janssens* had recently reduced its already infrequent sailings for Singapore, which caused some delay, but finally, toward the end of March, I embarked for Sampit. I was glad to see the controleur, who came down to the pier, for the rare occasions when steamers call here are almost festive events, and arrangements were at once made for my journey to Sembulo. At Pembuang we took on board the native kapala of the district, who was to accompany me; he also brought an attendant, a cook, and a policeman, all natives. Twelve hours later, when we arrived at the kampong Sembulo, the kapala who came on board the *Selatan* informed us that no Dayaks were there. As the lake was low and the water continued to fall it was impossible to proceed to Bangkal, the other kampong, or to remain here more than a few days. Therefore, at my request the native authorities agreed to have the Bangkal Dayaks congregate here, the kapala himself undertaking to bring them.

The population of the kampong Sembulo, formerly called Pulau Tombak, at the present time is Malay, comprising more than two hundred full-grown men, nearly all recent arrivals from Bandjermasin, Sampit, Pembuang, and other places. Very little rice is planted because the soil is sandy and unsuited to cultivation, therefore the inhabitants confine their activities mainly to rubber gathering. At that time about a hundred men were busy in the jungle on the opposite side, gathering white rubber, which is plentiful in the surrounding country. They cross the lake in their small prahus, pole them up the streams, and remain perhaps three months in the utan working under adverse conditions. When engaged in their pursuit they must always stand in water, which covers the ground and is usually shallow but at times reaches to the arm-pit.

Four weeks previously an epidemic of beri-beri had started with a mortality of one or two every day. When attacked by the disease they return to the kampong but only few recover, most of them dying from one or the other of the two forms of beri-beri. Nevertheless, the remainder continue the work undismayed—"business going on as usual." In the tropics life and death meet on friendly terms. "That is a sad phase of this country," said a Briton to me in India; "you shake hands with a man to-day and attend his funeral to-morrow."

At its deepest part the lake measures about seven metres. From May to August, when the Pembuang River is small and the lake is low, the depth is reduced to a metre. People then must walk far out to get water. Every afternoon we had gales accompanied by heavy rain from the northeast, although once it came from the southwest, and the *Selatan* had to put out another anchor. I was told that similar storms are usual every afternoon at that season (April), during which prahus do not venture out; apparently they also occur around Sampit and are followed by calm nights.

Eighteen Dayaks were brought here from Bangkal. Of these, nine were Tamoan, the tribe of the region, eight Katingan, and one Teroian (or Balok) from Upper Pembuang. They were measured, photographed, and interviewed. One man looked astonishingly like a Japanese.

The name of the tribe, Tamoan, also pronounced Samoan, means to wash. The tatu marks are the same as those of the Katingans. At present these natives have only six kampongs, three of them above Sampit. Cultivating rice was very difficult, they complained, on account of the poor soil and wet weather. The lake has few fish and they cannot be caught except when the water is low. There are no large serpents here, and neither snakes, dogs, nor crocodiles are eaten; but the rusa is accepted as food. Fruits, as the durian and langsat, are rather scarce.

Fire is made by twirling, and these natives use the sumpitan. They know how to make tuak, crushing the rice, boiling it, and then pouring it into a gutshi until the vessel is half full, the remaining space being filled with water. In three days the product may be drunk, but sometimes it is allowed to stand a month, which makes it much stronger. If there is no tuak there can be no dancing, they said. Many remarked upon the expense of obtaining a wife, the cost sometimes amounting to several hundred florins, all of which must be earned by gathering rubber. The tiwah feast is observed, but as to legends there are none, and their language and customs are disappearing.

These Tamoans are disintegrating chiefly on account of the ravages of cholera. About forty years previously an epidemic nearly extinguished Bangkal, and there was another in 1914. The result is that the population has changed, people from other kampongs, at times from other tribes, taking the places of the dead. At the kampong Sembulo there appear to be no Tamoans remaining, the Malays having easily superseded them.

Although my journey to the lake yielded no evidence to substantiate the legend connected with it, because I found no Dayaks left "to tell the tale," still, satisfaction is derived even from a negative result. Having accomplished what was possible I returned to Sampit, arriving almost at the same time a sailing ship came in from Madura, the island close to northeastern Java. It was of the usual solid type, painted white, red, and green, and loaded with obi, a root resembling sweet potatoes, which on the fourth day had all been sold at retail. A cargo of terasi, the well-known spicy relish made from crawfish and a great favourite with Malays and Javanese, was then taken on board.

In the small prison of Sampit, which is built of ironwood, the mortality from beri-beri among the inmates was appalling. Nine men, implicated in the murder of two Chinese traders, in the course of eight months while the case was being tried, all died except a Chinaman who was taken to Bandjermasin. I understood a new prison was about to be erected. It seems improbable that ironwood has any connection with this disorder, but Mr. Berger, manager of the nearby rubber plantation, told me the following facts, which may be worth recording: Six of his coolies slept in a room with ironwood floor, and after a while their legs became swollen in the manner which indicates beri-beri. He moved them to another room, gave them katjang idju, the popular vegetable food, and they soon recovered. He then replaced the ironwood floor with other material, and after that nobody who slept in the room was affected in a similar way.

I met in Sampit three Dayaks from the upper country of the Katingan on whom the operation of incision had been performed. According to reliable reports this custom extends over a wide area of the inland, from the upper regions of the Kapuas, Kahayan, and Barito Rivers in the east, stretching westward as far as and including the tribes of the Kotawaringin. Also, in the Western Division on the Upper Kapuas and Melawi Rivers, the same usage obtains. In Bandjermasin prominent Mohammedans, one of them a Malay Hadji, told me that the Malays also practise incision instead of circumcision. The Malays, moreover, perform an operation on small girls, which the Dayaks do not.

The controleur invited me to take part in a banquet which he gave to celebrate the completion of a road. There were present Malay officials, also Chinamen, and one Japanese. The latter, who arrived at Sampit one and a half years before with forty florins, had since increased his capital to a thousand through the sale of medicines to natives whom he reached by going up the rivers. We were seated at three tables, twenty-eight guests. The natives were given viands in addition to the menu provided, because they must have rice. Their women had helped to cook—no small undertaking for so many in an out-of-the-way place like Sampit. It was an excellent dinner; such tender, well-prepared beef I had not enjoyed for a long time. Claret, apollinaris, and beer were offered, the latter appearing to be the favourite. Women were served in another room after the men had dined.

FOLKLORE OF SOME OF THE TRIBES IN DUTCH BORNEO VISITED BY THE AUTHOR

1. THE MOTHERLESS BOY

(From the Penyahbongs, kampong Tamaloë)

Ulung Tiung was left at home by his father who went out hunting. Borro, the cocoanut-monkey, came and asked for food, but when Ulung gave him a little he refused to eat it and demanded more. The boy, who was afraid of him, then gave more, and Borro ate until very little remained in the house. The monkey then said, "I am afraid of your father, and want to go home." "Go," replied the boy, "but return again." When the father came home in the evening he was angry that the food had been taken.

The following day when the father went out hunting, Borro again came asking for food. The boy, at first unwilling, finally yielded; the monkey ate with much gusto and as before wanted to go home. "Do not go," said the boy, "my father is far away." "I smell that he is near," said Borro, and went.

When the father returned in the evening and saw that the food again had been eaten he was very angry with the boy, who replied: "Borro ate it—I did not take any." Whereupon the father said: "We will be cunning; next time he comes tell him I have gone far away.

381

Make a swing for him near your mat, and when he is in it tie rattan around him and swing him."

The father went away and the monkey came again and asked for food, and got it. When he had eaten the boy said: "You had better get into the swing near my mat." Borro liked to do that and seated himself in it, while the boy tied rattan around him and swung him. After a little while the monkey, fearing that the father might come back, said he wanted to get out, but the boy replied, "Father is not coming before the evening," at the same time tying more rattan around him, and strongly, too.

The father came home and fiercely said: "You have been eating my food for two days." Thereupon he cut off Borro's head, and ordered his son to take him to the river, clean him, and prepare the flesh to be cooked. The boy took Borro's body to the river, opened it and began to clean it, but all the small fish came and said: 'Go away! What you put into the water will kill us." The boy then took the monkey some distance off and the big fish came and said: "Come nearer, we want to help you eat him."

The sisters of Borro now arrived, and his brothers, father, children, and all his other relatives, and they said to Ulung Tiung: "This is probably Borro." "No," he said, "this is a different animal." Then the monkeys, believing what he said, went away to look for Borro, except one of the monkey children, who remained behind, and asked: "What are you doing here?" "What a question!" the boy answered; "I am cutting up this animal, Borro."

The child then called all the monkeys to return, and they captured Ulung Tiung and carried him to their house and wanted to kill him. "Don't kill me," he said, "I can find fruit in the utan." The monkeys permitted him to do that, and told him to return in the evening, but the boy said that first he would have to dream.

In the morning the monkeys asked him what he had dreamed. "There is plenty of fruit in the mountain far away," he answered, pointing afar, and all the monkeys went out to the mountain leaving their wives and children behind. When they were all gone Ulung Tiung killed the women and children with a stick, and went home to his father. "I killed the women and children," he declared, "but the men had not come back." "We will watch for them with sumpitan," said his father, and when the monkeys returned and found that all who had remained at home were dead, they began to look for Ulung Tiung, but he and his father killed half of them with sumpitan and the rest ran away.

NOTE.—Ulung Tiung is the name for a boy whose mother is dead, but whose father is alive. For the sake of convenience I have maintained the Malay name "borro" for the cocoanut-monkey.

2. THE FATHERLESS BOY

(From the Penyahbongs; kampong Tamaloë)

Ulung Ela made a fish-trap and when he returned next morning he found it full of fish. He put them in his rattan bag, which he slung on his back and started for home. As he walked, he heard an antoh, Aaton Kohang, singing, and he saw many men and women, to whom he called out: "It is much better you come to my place and sing there." Aaton Kohang said: "Very well, we will go there." The boy continued his march, and when he came home he gave one fish to his mother to roast, which she wrapped in leaves and put on the live coals. He also prepared fish for himself, ate quickly, and begged his mother to do the same. The mother asked: "Why do you hurry so?" The boy, who did not want to tell her that he had called an antoh, then said that it was not necessary to hurry.

After they had finished eating, in the evening Aaton Kohang arrived with many men and many women. They tickled the mother and her boy under the arms until they could not talk any more and were half dead, took what remained of the fish, and went away. The two fell asleep, but ants bit them in the feet and they woke up and saw that all the fish were gone. "Ha!" they said: "Aaton Kohang did this," and they ran away.

NOTE.—Ulung Ela is the name for a boy whose father is dead, but whose mother is alive.

3. THE TWO ORPHANS

(From the Penyahbongs; kampong Tamaloë)

Two small sisters, whose father and mother had died, went with the women to look for sago. The tree was cut and the sago, after having been beaten, was put into the large rattan bag. The younger child, who was sitting close to the bag, dropped asleep and fell into it. The other girl came to look for her sister but could not find her. She had disappeared, and when the women saw that the bag was already full they all went home. On returning next day they found plenty of sago inside of the tree, and had no difficulty in filling their bags.

NOTE.—Ulung Ania is the name for the elder of the two girl orphans. Ulung Kabongon is the name for the younger. When her elder sister died the latter became obon, and her name became Obon Kabongon.

4. THE TREE OF WHICH ANTOH IS AFRAID

(From the Penyahbongs; kampong Tamaloë)

Tabédjeh wanted to go to the place where a girl, Inyah, was living. On the way he met an antoh in the shape of a man with whom he began talking. Antoh said: "I am going to catch Inyah and eat her." Tabédjeh then drew his parang and cut off his head. But a new head grew, and many more, so that Tabédjeh became afraid and fled, with antoh running after him. He lost his parang, then, after a while, he stopped and took sticks to strike antoh with, but every time he struck the stick was wrested from him, and he had to take flight again.

He ran up on a mountain and antoh, in close pursuit, caught up with him sitting on a fallen tree. Tabédjeh was tired and short of breath, but when antoh saw what kind of a tree he was sitting on he said: "You may remain there. I cannot eat you now because I am afraid of that tree." Tabédjeh took a piece of the wood of the tree, which is called klamonang, and he went to the house of Inyah to show her the tree of which antoh is afraid, and they had their wedding at once.

5. LEAVES THAT BAFFLED ANTOH
(From the Penyahbongs; kampong Tamaloë)

Two brothers were walking in the utan, with sumpitans, when they met a pig which one of them speared. The quarry became furious and attacked the other one, but they helped each other and killed the pig, ate what they wanted, and continued their hunting.

Next they met a rhino which they killed. As they began to take off the hide, cutting into his chest, the rhino became alive again, and the hide turned out to be the bark of a tree. The two ran home, but the rhino came after them, so they again had to flee, pursued by him, until they came across a small tree called mora, of which antoh is afraid. They gathered some of the leaves, and as soon as the rhino saw that he ran away.

6. PENGANUN, THE HUGE SERPENT
(From the Penyahbongs; kampong Tamaloë)

The mother of Daring's wife ordered him to go out and hunt for animals to eat, but said they would have to be without bones. He searched for a month, and all that he got had bones. Finally he brought back a leech, which she ate. Then she said: "Go and look for penganun," the huge serpent with the golden horn. He met the monster and used all his poisoned darts before it succumbed. He left it there and went home. "Have you got the big serpent?" she asked him. "Yes!" he answered. She then went out to bring it in, but she cut off only a little of the flesh, which she brought back. It was cooked in bamboo, and the people in the house ate it, but before they had finished the meal they became crazy—fifteen of them. The affected ones, as well as the bamboo in which the cooking had been done, turned into stone, but the meat disappeared. Daring and his wife, who had not partaken of the meal, escaped.

NOTE.—There exists in Borneo a huge python, in Malay called sahua, which is the basis for a superstitious belief in a monster serpent, called penganun, the forehead of which is provided with a straight horn of pure gold. The tale is possibly influenced by Malay ideas. The Penyahbongs have a name for gold, bo-an, but do not know how to utilise the metal.

7. HOW THE PENGANUN WAS CAUGHT ALIVE
(From the Penyahbongs; kampong Tamaloë)

Two young girls, not yet married, went to fish, each carrying the small oblong basket which the Penyahbong woman is wont to use when fishing, holding it in one hand and passing it through the water. A very young serpent, of the huge kind called penganun, entered a basket and the child caught it and placed it on the bark tray to take it home.

Penganun ate all the fish on the tray, and the girls kept it in the house, catching fish for it, and it remained thus a long time. When it grew to be large it tried to eat the two girls, and they ran away to their mother, who was working on sago, while their father was sleeping near by. Penganun was pursuing them, and he caught the smaller one around the ankle, but the father killed the monster with his sumpitan and its spear point. With his parang he cut it in many pieces and his wife cooked the meat in bamboo, and they all ate it.

NOTE.—Penganun, see preceding tale. The sumpitan (blow-pipe) has a spear point lashed to one end, and thus also may serve as a spear.

8. THE FATHERLESS BOY

(From the Saputans; kampong Data Láong)

A woman was going to the ladang in the morning, and she said to her young son, Amon Amang, whose father was dead: "When the sun comes over the tree there you must begin to husk paddi." She then went away to the ladang while the boy remained at home. He carried the paddi, as well as the oblong wooden mortar, up into a tree. There he began to work, and the mortar and the paddi and the boy all tumbled down because the branch broke. A man helped the half-dead boy to come to his senses again, throwing water on him, and when the mother returned she was very angry to see the mortar broken and the paddi strewed all about. "I told you to husk paddi in the house when the sun came over the tree," she said. "Better that you now go and hunt birds."

The boy then decided to hunt. He climbed a tree and put up snares to catch birds. He caught a great many big hornbills, which he fastened alive to his loin cloth, and they began to fly, carrying the boy with them to a big tree, where they loosened themselves from him, left him in a cleft, and all flew away. The tree was very tall, but he climbed down a fig tree which grew beside it, descended to the ground, and went home.

His mother was not pleased that he did not bring any birds, and he told her what had happened. "Why all this?" she said. "You fell from the tree! You should have killed the birds," she declared reproachfully.

NOTE.—Amon Amang means the husband's child. (Amon = father; Amang = child.

During my stay of two weeks at Data Lahong fortunate circumstances enabled me to gather a considerable number of Saputan tales. Several prominent men from neighbouring kampongs visited me and were willing to tell them, while of equal importance was the fact that a Mohammedan Murung Dayak in my party spoke the language well and made a very satisfactory interpreter.

On the other hand, I remained among the Penihings for many weeks, but the difficulty of finding either men who knew folklore or who could interpret well, prevented me from securing tales in that tribe. However, there is strong probability that much of the folklore told me by the Saputans originated with the Penihings, which is unquestionably the case with No. 16, "Laki Mae." The reason is not far to seek since the Saputans appear to have been governed formerly by the Penihings, though they also are said to have had many fights with them. According to information given me at Long Tjehan, Paron, the Raja Besar in the kampong, until recent years was also raja of the Saputans.

9. THE ANTOH WHO MARRIED A SAPUTAN

(From the Saputans; kampong Data Láong)

Dirang and his wife, Inyah, went out hunting with dogs, and got one pig. She then cut rattan to bind the pig for carrying it home, and the man in tying, broke the rattan. He became very angry and told his wife to look for another piece of rattan. She went away and met an antoh in the shape of a woman who asked her: "Where are you going?" "To look for rattan," was the answer, and "What is your name?" Inyah asked. "I am Inyah Otuntaga," the antoh answered. Inyah then said: "Take this rattan and give it to my husband."

Inyah Otuntaga brought the rattan to the man, who tied the babi all around, and she took it up and carried it home. The man, meanwhile, followed her, thinking it was his wife. She went to this side and that side in the jungle, frequently straying. "What is the matter," he said, "don't you know the way?" "Never mind," she retorted, "I forgot." Arriving at the house she went up the wrong ladder, and the man was angry and said: "Don't you know the right ladder?" She answered: "I cannot get up the ladder." "Come up and walk in," he exclaimed, and began to think she was an antoh.

She entered the room and slept there, lived with him ever after, and had two children. His former wife, much incensed, went to the house of her father, and after a while she had a child. Her little boy chanced to come to the house of his father, who asked his name. "I am the son of Inyah," he said. Then the father learned where his former wife was, and he went to fetch her, and afterward both wives and their children lived together.

10. LAKI SORA AND LAKI IYU
(From the Saputans; kampong, Data Láong)

Two men, Sora and Iyu, went into the utan to hunt with sumpitans. While Iyu made a hut for the two, Sora went to look for animals and came across a pig, which he killed. He brought the liver and the heart to the hut and gave them to Iyu to cook. When the cooking was finished Iyu advised him of it, and the two sat down to eat. It was already late in the afternoon and Iyu, whose duty it was to fetch the pig, waited until next day, when he went away to bring it in, but instead he ate it all by himself, and then returned to the hut and told Sora what he had done. It was now late in the evening and they both went to sleep.

The following morning Sora went out again with his sumpitan, but chased all day without meeting an animal, so he took one root of a water-plant called keládi, as well as one fruit called pangin, and went home. The keládi was roasted, but the fruit it was not necessary to prepare. They then sat down to eat, but could not satisfy their hunger, and Iyu was angry and asked why he brought so little. "I did not bring more," Sora answered, "because it is probable the owner would have been angry if I had." Iyu said: "To-morrow I shall bring plenty."

Next morning Iyu came to the place where Sora had found the root and the fruit, and he ate all that remained there, but this belonged to an antoh, called Amenaran, and one of his children saw Iyu eat the root which he did not cook, and also saw him climb the tree and eat the fruit. He went and told his father, the antoh, who became angry, spoke to Iyu about it, and wanted to know who had given him permission.

Iyu, who was up in the tree still gorging himself with fruit, said he was not afraid and he would fight it out that evening. Amenaran stood below and lightning poured forth from his mouth and thunder was heard. Iyu said: "I have no spear, nor parang, but I will kill that antoh." And the big pig he had eaten and all the roots and all the fruits that he had been feeding on, an immense quantity of fæces, he dropped on Amenaran's head, and it killed him. Iyu returned home and told Sora that he had put Amenaran to death. They then went out and killed many animals with the sumpitan and returned to the kampong. "Now that antoh is dead we can no more eat raw meat nor much fruit," said Iyu.

Long ago it was the custom to eat the meat raw and much of it, as well as much fruit, and one man alone would eat one pig and a whole garden. Now people eat little. With the death of antoh the strong medicine of the food is gone, and the Saputans do not eat much.

NOTE.—Laki is the Malay word for man or male, adopted by many of the tribes. The native word for woman, however, is always maintained. Keládi is a *caladium*, which furnishes the principal edible root in Borneo.

11. THE WONDERFUL TREE

(From the Saputans; kampong Data Láong)

Tanipoi bore a female infant, and when the child had been washed with water on the same day, the father gave her the name Aneitjing (cat). Years passed, and the girl had learned to bring water in the bamboo and to crush paddi. And the mother again became pregnant, and in due time had another little girl which was called Inu (a kind of fruit).

Now, among the Saputans the custom long ago was that the woman who had a child should do no work during forty days. She must not bring water, nor husk paddi, nor cook. She remained in the house and took her bath in the river daily. She slept much and ate pork cooked in bamboo, and rice, if there was any, and she was free to eat anything else that she liked. Her husband, Tanuuloi, who during this time had to do all the work, became tired of it, and he said to his wife: "I cannot endure this any longer. I would rather die."

After he had cooked the meal and they had eaten
he said: "Take the two children and go with me to the
river." All four of them went into a prahu which he
paddled down stream until they came to a large rock
in the middle of the river, where he stopped it. They
all climbed on the rock, and the prahu he allowed to
drift away. He then said to his wife: "You and I will
drown ourselves." "I cannot," she said, "because I
have a small child to suckle." He then tore the child
from the mother's breast and placed it on the rock. The
two children and the mother wept, and he caught hold
of one of her hands, dragged her with him into the water,
and they were both drowned.

The two children remained on the rock all day.
After sunset Deer (rusa) arrived. The older child called
out: "Take me from here." And Deer came to the stone
and placed Aneitjing on his back, and behind her Inu,
and carried them ashore. Deer then made a clearing
in the utan and built a hut for them. He then went to
the ladang to look for food, but before starting he said
to the children: "I am going to the ladang. Maybe I
shall be killed by the dogs. In that case you must take
my right arm and my right eye and bring them here."

Deer went away and was attacked by dogs. The
two children heard the barking, and when they arrived
the dogs were gone and Deer was found dead. The children took the right arm and the right eye and went home,
made a clearing and dug a hole, where the arm and the
eye were placed, and they covered the hole with earth.
They often went to look at that place. After twenty

days they saw a sprout coming up, and in twenty years
this had grown into a big tree which bore all sorts of fruit
and other good things. From the tree fell durian, nangka,
and many other kinds of delicious fruit, as well as clothing, spears, sumpitans, gongs, and wang (money).

Rumour of this spread to the kampong, and two men
arrived, Tuliparon, who was chief, and his brother Semor-
ing. They had heard of the two young women, and they
made a hut for themselves near by, but did not speak
to the girls. They went to sleep and slept day after
day, a whole year, and grass grew over them. Inu, the
younger, who was the brighter of the two, said to Aneitjing: "Go and wake these men. They have been sleeping a long time. If they have wives and children in the
kampong this will make much trouble for all of them."
Aneitjing then asked Tipang Tingai for heavy rain. It
came in the evening and flooded the land, waking the
two men who found themselves lying in the water. They
placed their belongings under the house of the women
and went to the river to bathe. They then returned
and changed their chavats under the house. The women
wanted to call to them, but they were bashful, so they
threw a little water down on them. The men looked up
and saw that there were women above and they ascended
the ladder with their effects.

The girls gave them food, and Tuliparon said to Inu:
"I am not going to make a long tale of it. If you agree
I will make you my wife, and if you do not agree, I will
still make you my wife." Inu answered: "Perhaps you
have a wife and children in the kampong. If you have,

I will not, but if you have not, then I will." "I am free," he said, "and have neither wife nor child." Reassured on this point she consented. His brother and Aneitjing agreed in the same way. The women said that they wanted always to live where they had the tree with so many good things. The men felt the same way, and they went to the kampong and induced all the people to come out there, and thus a new kampong was founded.

NOTE.—Tipang Tingai means the highest God, the same as the Malay Tuan Allah. It is also used by the Penyahbongs.

12. MOHAKTAHAKAM WHO SLEW AN ANTOH

(From the Saputans; kampong Data Láong)

Once upon a time three brothers, Mohaktahakam, Batoni, and Bluhangoni, started in the morning from the kampong and walked to another kampong where Pahit, an antoh, had a fish-trap. They were intent on stealing the fish, and as they went along they considered among themselves how they could take it. Pahit was very strong, but Mohaktahakam said: "Never mind, I am going to fight it out with him." Arriving there they let the water out of the trap, and with parang and spear they killed lots of fish of many kinds, filling their rattan bags with them. Taking another route they hurried homeward. Their burdens were heavy, so they could not reach the kampong, but made a rough shelter in the usual way on piles, the floor being two or three feet above the ground. They cut saplings and quickly made a framework, called tehi, on which the fish were placed. Underneath they made a big fire which smoked and cured them. In the morning they had boiled rice and fish to eat, and then went out to hunt for animals with sumpitan. The fish meanwhile remained on the tehi, the fire being kept alive underneath.

Pahit found his trap dry and no fish there. "Why have people been bold enough to take the fish?" he said to himself. "They don't know I am strong and brave"; and, very angry, he followed their tracks. He had gone scarcely half-way when he smelled the fish, which was very fat. When he arrived at the camp he found the fish over the fire, but nobody there. He gathered some leaves together behind the camp and sat down upon them to wait the arrival of the men.

In the afternoon Batoni and Bluhangoni returned to camp carrying much pig and deer. He immediately caught hold of both of them, lifted them up and brought them down with force upon the rough floor of the hut, and both died. Pahit saw that places had been made for three men to sleep, and knowing that there must be another man coming he decided to wait. The two bodies he placed under the hut, on the ground. After a while Mohaktahakam came, carrying pig, deer, rhino, wild ox, and bear, and threw it all down near the drying fish, to cook it later. He was tired, having walked all day, and went up into the hut to smoke tobacco. Pahit saw this and went after him. He caught hold of the man to throw him down, but could not lift him. Mohakta-hakam, very angry, caught Pahit by the arms, lifted him up, threw him against the floor and killed him.

"Pahit spoke of being strong and brave, but I am stronger," he said.

Mohaktahakam then made his brothers come to life again, and they cleaned all the animals they had caught and placed the meat on a tehi to dry and smoke. Then they cooked meat in bamboo and ate, afterward going to sleep. During the night one of them at times mended the fire, which was kept burning. In the morning, after eating, they went home to the kampong, carrying bags full of meat and fish.

NOTE.—Tehi, a framework for drying fish or meat, is called in Malay, salai.

13. THE MAGIC BABI BONE
(From the Saputans; kampong Data Láong)

Dirang left the kampong to hunt for heads, with three prahus and many men, armed with parangs, shields, sumpitans, and spears, and they also carried some rice for provisions. After a while the people who remained behind became very hungry, and one day Inyah, the wife of Dirang, went out to look for bamboo shoots to eat. She met a small babi (pig), caught it, and brought it home. In the kampong she asked the men to help her make a shed for it.

The babi, which was male, grew bigger and bigger. It was very strong, and when dogs, cats, or hens came near the shed it would kill and eat them. It was fierce and angry because it had not enough to eat, and finally it turned the shed over and killed and ate all the people. No one escaped but Inyah, who fled to another kampong, where she asked for help and the people permitted her to remain there.

Shortly afterward the babi arrived. All the people heard the noise it made as it came through the utan, breaking the jungle down. They said to Inyah: "You would better run away from here. We are afraid he may eat us." Inyah went away, trying to reach another kampong. She got there and asked for help against the man-eating babi. Hardly had she received permission to remain before a great noise was heard from the babi coming along. The people, frightened, asked her to pass on, and she ran to another kampong. There was a woman kapala in that kampong who lived in a house that hung in the air. Inyah climbed the ladder, which was drawn up after her. The babi came and saw Inyah above, but could not reach her, and waited there many days.

Dirang, who was on his way back from the head-hunting expedition, came down the river, and he said to one of his companions: "It is well to stop here and make food." This chanced to be close to the place where Inyah was. They went ashore to make camp. Some of them went out to search for wood and met the babi, who attacked them, and they fled to their prahus. When Dirang, who was an antoh, saw his men on the run, he became very angry, went after the babi, and cut off its head. His men cut up the body and cooked the meat in bamboo, near the river, sitting on a long, flat rock. They ate much, and Dirang said that he now wanted to paddle down to the kampong, so they all started. Inyah had seen

Dirang, and she said to the woman kapala: "Look! There is my husband. No other man would have been brave enough to kill the babi." The woman kapala said: "I should like to have such a husband if I wanted one, but I am afraid of a husband." Inyah said: "I want to go down." And she walked over to the place where the men had been sitting on the rock, went upon it, and accidentally stepped on a bone left from the meal, which hit her on the inside of the right ankle. The bone was from the right hind leg of the babi, and was sharp, so it drew a little blood from the ankle.

She felt pain and went back to the house. Some time later the leg began to swell, and as time passed it grew bigger and bigger. The woman kapala said: "There must be a child inside." "If that is the case," said Inyah, "then better to throw it away." "No, don't do that. Wait until the child is born and I will take care of it," said the kapala. When her time had come the child arrived through the wound made by the babi bone, and the kapala washed the child and took care of it. When two months old the child was given the name Obongbadjang. When he was fifteen years old he was as strong as Dirang.

Dirang had brought many heads to the kampong, but finding all the people dead and houses fallen down, he became angry and killed the slaves he had brought back. He then went out on another hunt for heads. When the prahus passed the kampong where Inyah was, all the people in the house saw them, and Obongbadjang, her young son, who had heard much of Dirang, went down to see him. "Where are you going?" asked Dirang. "I want to go with you," answered the boy. Dirang liked him, and let him into the prahu.

They travelled far and wide, and finally came to the kampong which they wanted to attack. Dirang went in from one end of the house and Obongbadjang from the other, and they cut the heads from all the people, men, women, and children, and met in the middle of the house. Dirang was wondering who this young man was who was strong like himself and not afraid. "My name is Obongbadjang," he said, "the son of Dirang and Inyah." He then ran away, although Dirang tried to keep him back, and he ran until he arrived where his mother was.

On seeing his son run away Dirang felt "sick in his throat," then collected all the heads, comprising the population of the whole kampong, put them in the prahus, and returned to look for his son and wife. He stopped at the same place where he had killed the big babi and made a hut. He then went to look for Obongbadjang and Inyah. When he was walking under the house, which was high up in the air, Inyah threw a little water down on him. He turned his head up and saw there was a house, but there was no ladder and he could not get up. They put out the ladder and he went up and met Inyah again, who, until then, he did not know was alive. He also met his son, and after remaining a little while he took them away to rebuild their kampong.

NOTE.—"Sick in his throat," Saputan mode of speech for deep emotional depression, is similar to our "feeling a choking in the throat." The Malays say: "Sick in his liver."

For the sake of convenience the Malay name babi for a pig, perfectly known to the Dayaks, has been maintained in this tale.

14. WHEN HUSBAND AND WIFE ARE ANTOHS
(From the Saputans; kampong Data Láong)

There were many young men who wanted to marry Inu Songbakim, a young girl, but she liked only one man, Monjang Dahonghavon, and, having obtained the consent of her father and mother, he shared her mat. One day he went out to work, making planks with his axe, while she remained at home cooking. When she had prepared the food she took it to him, and when she arrived at the place where he was working he looked at her as he was cutting with the axe and hurt himself. He died, and his father came and took the corpse to the house. Being an antoh he restored the life of his son, who became very angry with his wife for being the cause of his death. He wanted to kill her, but as she was very strong he could not do it, and instead, with his parang, killed her father and mother. His wife, in turn, became filled with wrath, and with a parang killed his father and mother.

The young man then left her to look for another wife, but could not find any that was to his liking, strong and good-looking, so after a while he decided to return to the wife he already had. "I like you much," she said, "but if you want to have me again you must make my father and mother alive again." "I will do that," he answered, "if you first will restore to life my father and mother." They were both antohs, so there was a general return to life, and the people from the two kampongs to which the families belonged came together and made the kampongs into one.

15. THE WOMAN, THE BIRD, AND THE OTTER
(From the Saputans; kampong Data Láong)

Many young men courted Ohing Blibiching, but she was difficult to please. Finally, she favoured Anyang Mokathimman because he was strong, skilful in catching animals, brave in head-hunting. She said: "Probably you have a wife." "No, I am alone," he said, and her father and mother having given consent, they then lived together.

After a while he said: "I want to go away and hunt for heads." She said: "Go, but take many men with you. If you should be sick, difficulties would be great." She then made rice ready in a basket, calculating that on a long journey they would depend more on the sago found in the utan. They would also kill animals for food, therefore, in addition to their parangs, the men took sumpitans along.

"If we have any mishaps," he said, "I shall be away two months. If not, I shall be back in a month." She remained in the kampong guarded by her father, mother, and other people, and after a while many young men began to pay her attention, telling her: "He has been away a long time. Maybe he will not return." One day at noon when she was filling her bamboo receptacles in the river as usual, taking a bath at the same time, she saw a fish sleeping, and caught it. She then lifted on her back the big-meshed rattan bag which held the bamboo receptacles, all full of water, and went home, carrying the fish in her hand. Before cooking it she went to husk paddi.

The bird Teong, who had heard she was beautiful, saw her and he liked her much. He flew to a tree from which he could get a good look at her where she was husking the paddi. In admiration he jumped from branch to branch until a dead one broke which fell down and wounded young Otter in the river under the tree. The mother of Otter became angry with Bird Teong for the injury. "I have been in this tree quite a while," Bird answered, "because I like to look at that woman. I did not know Otter was underneath. If you want damages, ask that woman there." "Why should I pay Otter?" the woman said. "I did not call Bird Teong. I have just finished pounding and am going to cook fish. This case we will settle to-morrow. I am hungry now." She went away and so did Bird and Otter. She cooked rice in one bamboo and the fish in another. Then she ate, after which she went to the river as the sun was setting, to take her bath. She soon went to sleep.

Early the next morning she made her usual tour to the river to bring water and take her bath, and when she had eaten, Bird and Otter arrived. Otter wanted damages from Bird, and Bird insisted that the woman should pay. She repeated that she knew nothing of Bird and had not asked him to come. As they were arguing, to her great relief her husband arrived. He brought many prisoners and many heads. "It is well you have come," she said. "Bird and Otter have made a case against me. I was husking paddi, and Bird liked to look at me. I did not know he was there in the tree for a long time. A branch fell down and wounded Otter's child,

making her very angry, and she asks damages from me."
"This case is difficult," the husband answered. "I must
think it over." After a while he said: "The best thing
to do is to give food to both." Bird was given fruit to
eat and Otter fish, and they went home satisfied. All
the people of the kampong gathered and rejoiced at
the successful head-hunting. They killed pigs and hens,
and for seven nights they ate and danced.

NOTE.—When an attack on men is decided upon the sumpitan is hidden
and left behind after the spear-head has been detached from it and tied to
a long stick. This improvised spear is the principal weapon on head-hunting raids, as well as on the chase after big game. The bird, called by the
Saputans teong, is common, of medium size, black with yellow beak, and
yellow around the eyes, also a little red on the head. It learns easily to
talk, and is also common in Java.

16. LAKI MAE
(From the Saputans; kampong Data Láong)

The wife of Laki Mae was pregnant and wanted to
eat meat, so she asked her husband to go out hunting.
He brought in a porcupine, wild hens, kidyang, pig, and
deer, and he placed all the meat on the tehi, to smoke
it over fire, that it should keep. But the right hind leg
of the porcupine was hung up by itself unsmoked, to
be eaten next day. They had their evening meal and
then went to sleep. In the night she bore an infant son,
and, therefore, next morning another woman came to
do the cooking. She took the hind leg and before proceeding to cook it, washed it. It slipped through a hole
in the floor to the ground underneath. Looking through
the hole she saw a small male child instead of the leg,
and she told Mae of this.

"Go and take this child up and bring it here. It is good luck," he said. "It is my child too." It was brought up to the room and washed and laid to the wife's breast, but the child would not suckle. Mae said: "It is best to give him a name now. Perhaps he will suckle then." He then asked the child if it wanted to be called Nonjang Dahonghavon, and the child did not. Neither did it want Anyang Mokathimman, nor Samoling, nor Samolang. It struck him that perhaps he might like to be called Sapit (leg) Tehotong which means "Porcupine Leg," and the child began to suckle at once. The child of the woman was given a name two months later, Lakin Kudyáng.

For two years the mother suckled the two, and then they were old enough to play behind the houses of the kampong. They saw many birds about, and they asked their father to give each of them a sumpitan. When they went out hunting the human boy got one bird, but the other boy got two. Next time the woman's son killed a plandok (mouse-deer), but the other one secured a pig. Their father was angry over this and said to "Porcupine Leg": "Go and kill the two old bears and bring the young ones here." He had recently seen two bears, with one cub each, under the roots of a tree in the neighbourhood. The boy went, and the bears attacked him and tried to bite him, but with his parang he killed both of them, and brought the cubs along to the kampong, bringing besides the two dead bears. The father again sent him out, this time to a cave where he knew there were a pair of tiger-cats and one cub. "Go and kill the

pair and bring the cub here," he said. Again the boy
was successful. Laki Mae did not like this and was
angry.

In the evening "Porcupine Leg" said to his brother:
"I have a long time understood that father is angry with
me. To-morrow morning I am going away. I am not
eating, and I will look for a place to die." His brother
began to weep, and said he would go with him. Next
morning they told their father they were going to hunt
for animals and birds. But when they did not return
in the evening, nor later, the mother said: "I think they
will not come back." Half a month later many men
attacked the kampong. Laki Mae fought much and
was tired. "If the boys had remained this would not
have happened," the people said angrily to him. In
the meantime the human son began to long to return,
and he persuaded "Porcupine Leg" to accompany him.
They both came back and helped to fight the enemy,
who lost many dead and retired.

NOTE.—This story is also found with the Penihings, from whom undoubtedly it is derived. *Laki*, see No. 10. *Tehi*, see No. 12.

17. SEMANG, THE BAD BOY
(From the Long-Glats; kampong Long Tujo)

A woman called Daietan had one child, Semang, who
was a bad boy. He was lazy, slept day and night, and
did not want to make ladang nor plant any banana nor
papaya trees. His mother angrily said to him: "Why
don't you exert yourself to get food?" Semang said:
"Well, I will go to-morrow to search for something to eat."

At sunrise next morning he went away in a prahu, paddling up-stream. He reached a kampong, and the name of the raja here was Anjangmaran. He could find no food, so he went on to the next kampong, and to another, but had no success, so he continued his journey, and then arrived at the fourth kampong. There were no people here. It was a large kampong with many houses, and grass was growing everywhere.

He went up into a room and there he found all sorts of goods; salt, gongs, many tempaians (large Chinese urns) in which paddi was stored, and tobacco. Semang said to himself, "I am rich. Here is all that I need." And he lay down to sleep. In the night Deer (rusa) arrived and called out: "Is there any one here?" He ascended the ladder and lay down near the cooking place. Semang heard him, but was afraid to move, and slept no more. In the night he heard Deer talk in his sleep: "To-morrow morning I am going to look for a small bottle with telang kliman. It is underneath the pole in front of the house."

Semang said: "Who is talking there?" Deer waked up and became frightened, ran down the ladder, and got into Semang's prahu, where he went to sleep. Before dawn Semang arose and walked down toward the prahu. On his way he saw an ironwood pole in front of the room, went up to it, and began to dig under it. He found a small bottle which he opened, and he put his first finger into it. He was astonished to see that his finger had become white, and he said: "This must be good to put on the body." He poured some into his hollowed hand and applied it all over his body and hair. His body became white and his clothes silken.

Pleased with this, Semang ascended the ladder, gathered together all the goods that he had found in the room, and began taking them to the prahu. There he found Deer asleep, and killed him with his spear. After bringing all the goods from the house to the prahu, Semang started down-stream. Owing to the magic liquid his prahu had become very large, and carried much, much goods, as well as the dead deer.

He travelled straight for the kampong, where he caught sight of his mother. "O, mother!" he cried, and went up the ladder carrying the bottle. He washed his mother with the liquid. She became young and beautiful, and it also gave her many beautiful garments. By the same aid Semang made the room handsome. Everything became changed instantly. The ceiling was of ironwood, and the planks of the floor were of a wood called lampong, which resembles cedar. Large numbers of brass vessels were there, and many gongs were brought from the prahu, besides a great quantity of various goods. The mother said: "This is well, Semang." She felt that she no longer had cause to be troubled; that whatever she and Semang might need would come without effort on their part.

Note.—According to Long-Glat belief, the deer, called in Malay rusa, possesses a magic liquid which enables it to restore the dead to life. The name of the liquid is telang kliman (telang = liquid; kliman = to make alive).

18. ADVENTURES IN PURSUIT OF MAGIC

(From the Long-Glats, kampong Long Tujo)

Once there lived a woman, Boamaring, who was Raja Besar in a large kampong where people did not know how to work. They could not make ladangs nor prahus. Everything they needed came to them of its own accord, and the rajas of the neighbouring kampongs were afraid of her. This is the way it came about.

She heard a rumour of a musical instrument which could play by itself, and which had the power of bringing all necessary food. She said to her husband, whose name was Batangnorang, "Go to the limit of the sky and bring the instrument that plays by itself." Putting on tiger skin, and carrying his parang and sumpitan, Batangnorang went into a small prahu which was able to fly, and it flew one month, to the end of the sky. He landed in a durian tree, near a small house covered with the tail feathers of the hornbill. Its walls were of tiger skins, the ridgepole, as well as the poles of the framework, were made of brass, and a carving of the naga stood out from each gable.

He heard music from inside the house, and saw a woman dancing alone to the tune of the instrument that played by itself. She was the antoh of the end of the sky, and he knew that she ate people, so he was afraid to come down, for many men since long ago had arrived there and had been eaten. Many corpses of men could be seen lying on the ground. From his bamboo cask he took a small arrow, placed it in his sumpitan, and then blew it out toward the dancing woman. The arrow hit the woman in the small of the back, and she fell mortally wounded. Then he flew down to the house, finished killing her with his spear, and cut her head off with his parang. He then went up to her room and took the musical instrument, her beautiful clothing, and beads, and placed all, together with the head, in his prahu. He also took many fine rattan mats, burned the house, and flew away in the sky. After a month he arrived in his kampong and returned to his wife. "Here is the musical instrument you wanted," he said. "Good!" she answered, "what else did you hunt for?"

He placed it on the floor and asked it to play by striking it one time. Sugar, boiled rice, durian, cocoanuts began to fall down, also tobacco, salt, clothing—all the good things that they could wish for. The Raja Besar was greatly pleased and was all smiles, and the people of her kampong no longer found it necessary to work. Everything that they needed came when they wished for it, and all enjoyed this state of things.

When a month had passed she learned of a woman's hair ornament which was to be found in the river far away. It was of pure gold, and when one hung it up and struck it all sorts of food would drop from it. "Go and get that," she told her husband. "It is in a cave underneath the waters of the river."

Batangnorang made himself ready. He put on tiger skin, placed on his head a rattan cap with many tail feathers of the hornbill fastened to it, took his parang, his shield adorned with human hair, and his sumpitan.

But he did not carry mats for bedding, nor food. He had only to wish for these things and they came. He then said farewell to his wife in a way that the Long-Glats use when departing on a long journey. She sat on the floor, and bending down he touched the tip of his nose to the tip of hers, each at the same time inhaling the breath as if smelling.

Batangnorang departed, stopping on the river bank, where he stood for a time looking toward the East, and calling upon the antoh Allatala. Then he went into the water, dived, and searched for ten days until he found the cave, inside of which there was a house. This was the home of the crocodile antoh, and was surrounded by men, some of them alive, some half dead, and many dead.

Crocodile was asleep in his room, and all was silent. Batangnorang went up on the gallery and sat down. After waiting a long time Crocodile awoke. He smelt man, went to the door which he opened a little, enough to ascertain what this was, and he saw Batangnorang. Then he passed through it and said to the stranger: "How did you come here? What is your name?" "I come from the earth above. I am Batangnorang." He was afraid antoh would eat him, and Crocodile's sister being his mother he added timidly: "I have a mother. I do not know of a father," he continued. "My mother, your sister, told me to go and meet my father down in the water." "What necessity was there for my child to come here?" asked Crocodile. "I am looking for a woman's hair ornament of gold," he answered. Crocodile said: "If you are my child then I will cook rice for you."

They both went into the room, which was fine, made of stone; the roof was of gold, and there were many gongs and much goods there. Crocodile cooked rice, but as he wanted to try the stranger he took one man from those outside, cut him into many pieces, and made a stew. He then told him to eat, and being afraid to do otherwise, Batangnorang ate it. Crocodile then said: "Truly you are my child. Another man would not have eaten this stew."

After the meal Crocodile put the remainder of the food away, with a tiny key opened a small steel trunk, took out the gold ornament, and gave it to Batangnorang. "Give this to your mother, Crocodile. When she wants to use it, hang it up and place a beautiful mat underneath. Then strike it one time with the first finger. Whatever you ask for must come."

Batangnorang took the hair ornament and placed it in the pocket of his shirt, put on his parang, and took his spear and shield. He then said farewell, and as he walked away he suddenly turned and thrust his spear into Crocodile's breast and killed him. Batangnorang carried away all that he desired, diamonds as large as hens' eggs, and much gold. He then went home, ascended to the room where his wife sat, and laid his weapons away.

He seated himself near his wife and produced the ornament. "I got this," and handed it to her. "How do you use it?" she asked. He hung it up by a string and placed a fine rattan mat underneath. All the people in the kampong gathered to see this, women, men, and children. He then struck it with his first finger, when lo! and behold! there fell all around pork, boiled rice, vegetable stew, sugar-cane, papaya, durian, bananas, pineapples, and white onions. All present ate as long as they were able, and food continued to fall. After that people slept at night and arose in the morning to eat and do no work, because all that they wished for was produced immediately.

NOTE.—The flying prahu, mentioned in this legend, plays an important part in the religious exercises of the Ot-Danum, Katingan, and Kahayan. See page 336. The head ornament of women is different in this tribe from those observed elsewhere in Borneo. It may be seen in the back view of the three Long-Glat women in Chapter XXVI. The tale shows Malay influence by such expressions as gold, diamonds, brass, shirt pocket, bottle. Allatala, the rendering of the Mahommedan Tuan Allah, is accepted as an antoh also by certain Dayak tribes in Southern Borneo. Steel trunks, as sold by Chinese or Malays, are much in favour with the Dayaks, and were observed wherever I travelled. It is one of the first articles that those who have taken part in an expedition to New Guinea will buy to take home. White onions are usually to be procured on travels among the Dayaks, and of course are not originally indigenous, no more than are sugarcane and pine-apples (both scarce, especially the latter), cassava and red peppers.

The non-Dayak expressions do not necessarily imply that the legend is Malay. The one circumstance that might lend colour to this belief is that in this legend, as well as in the preceding (Semang), both of which were told me by the same man, the beauty of idle life is glorified. This seems to be more a Malay than a Dayak quality. I was not long enough among the Long-Glats to be able to decide on this point. Circumstances favour a non-Malay origin. My informant, the kapala of Long Tujo, who showed Malay influence (see page 272), may have embellished his narrative by his acquired knowledge of things foreign. He was in reality a thorough Dayak, and he had scruples about telling me these stories. He hesitated, especially in regard to the one related, because it might injure him much to let me know that one. The Long-Glat leave-taking, described, is called *ngebaw* (to smell) *laung* (nose).

19. THE ORANG-UTAN AND THE DAYAK

(From the Ot-Danums; kampong Gunong Porok, Upper Kahayan River)

There was a man who, in grief and sorrow over the death of his wife, his children, and others, left his house and went far into the utan. Feeling tired he lay down to rest under a great lanan tree. While he slept a female orang-utan, which had its nest in the same tree and had been away hunting for food, came home, lifted the man in her arms, and carried him to her nest high up in the branches. When he awoke it seemed impossible for him to climb down, so he remained there. Each day she brought him fruit of various kinds, also occasionally boiled rice, stolen from the houses of the ladangs. After a few days she began to take liberties with him. At first the man declined her advances and she became angry, showing her teeth and nails. Finally she bit him in the shoulder, and then he surrendered. The man remained in the tree over a year. Although anxious to escape he feared the revenge of the orang-utan too much to make the attempt. In due time a male child was born who was human, but covered with long hair.

One day when she was absent seeking food he saw a sailing ship approach the coast and put out a boat for hauling water from the river near by. Hastily stringing his garments together he began the descent, but the rope was not long enough; however, by letting himself drop part of the distance he succeeded in getting down, and went away in the boat. Not finding him at home the orang-utan tried to swim to the ship, but the distance was too great. She then ascended the tree, and, in full view of the ship as it sailed away, she lifted the child and tore it in twain.

NOTE.—The Dayaks insist that this animal can swim, and my informant, a trustworthy Kahayan, said he had seen it. The orang-utan spends most of his time in the trees, seldom descending to the ground. That the one in this case is assumed to follow the daily habit of the Dayak is in accordance with the spirit of folk-lore.

20. BRANAK, THE ANTOH

(From the Ot-Danums, of the Upper Kahayan River)

A man called Mai Boang (father of Boang) had a very good-looking son who owned a fine big male dog, and when the child grew to be old enough he used the animal for hunting. One day when the dog was following the tracks of a deer he came into a long, long cave and Boang followed. To pass through the cave consumed thrice the time required to cook rice. Emerging on the other side the dog and the boy arrived at a house where there was a handsome woman. As darkness was falling he asked if he might stay over night, and she gave permission, the dog remaining under the house. Each was attracted by the other, so they passed the night together. Boang remained there, and in time she bore him a son. She possessed a female dog, and the two dogs had two male and two female pups.

Two or three years later Boang wanted to see his father and mother. She said: "I will go with you for a short time." With wife and child he went away, but he soon had to return because she did not like his country, of which the language and everything else was different.

They came back, lived long, and had many children. Her name was Kamkamiak and she had long, long nails. When he was disinclined to comply with her wishes she forced him by using her nails on a tender spot. She shows herself to-day as alang, the black hawk.

The descendants of this pair are also Kamkamiak, evil antohs of women at childbirth. The offspring of the dogs is another kind of antoh, called Penyakit (sickness). One of these appears in the form of a large goat which is seen only occasionally. It bites in the neck and the throat, the wounds are invisible, and the victim must die on the second or third day.

When the descendants of Mai Boang are ill they become better when relating the story of Boang.

NOTE.—The handsome woman who figures in this story is an evil antoh which afflicts women at childbirth and by the Ot-Danums and others is called Kamkamiak, the one with the long nails. She is also commonly known by the name Branak. She causes the woman to lose much blood and to have pain in the uterus, the nails of the antoh playing an important part in these conditions. Men who work in the utan gathering rubber, rattan, etc., are liable to get a disorder under the scrotum that looks like scratches, and which ulcerate and may be troublesome for several months or a year. These are ascribed to the long nails of the antoh, Branak, and sacrifices of sugar and eggs are offered.

Pontianak, the well-known town in the Western Division of Dutch Borneo, is the name of another good-looking female antoh, who causes injury to women at childbirth.

Some evil antohs, by Kahayans and others called kuyang, also select maternity victims. They are believed to fly through the air at night, appearing like fireflies, and enter the woman through head, neck, or stomach, doing much harm. They are supposed to suck blood, and when a woman dies at childbirth from bleeding, the belief is that it was caused by these evil spirits that in the daytime appear as ordinary human beings. They are also able to suck blood from men and kill them. The goat is at times an antoh, as is also the case with the water-buffalo, which may appear in dreams and cause illness.

The period of time required for "cooking rice" mentioned in the tale is called one pemasak, equal to about half an hour.

21. THE PÁTIN FISH

(From the Katingans; kampong Talinka)

A Dayak went fishing and caught a pátin which he took home in his prahu. He left the fish there and advised his wife, who went to fetch it. Upon approach she heard the crying of an infant, the fish having changed into a child, and she took it up, brought it home, gave it to eat and drink, and clothed it. The little one proved to be a girl who grew to womanhood, married, and had children. She said to her husband: "As long as we are married you must never eat pátin."

After a time the husband saw another man catch a pátin, and feeling an irresistible desire to eat the fat, delicious-looking fish, he was presented with a portion which he took to his house and cooked. Seeing this, his wife for the second time said: "Why do you eat pátin? You do not like me." "I must have this," he said, and he ate, and also gave it to his children to eat. "I am not human," she said, "I am pátin, and now I will return to the water. But mind this: If you or your descendants ever eat pátin you will be ill." And she went down to the river and became fish again. Since that time her descendants do not eat pátin, even when they accept Islam. Some have dared to break the rule, and they have become ill with fever and diarrhœa, accompanied by eruptions, abscesses, and open sores on the arms and legs. The remedy is to burn the bones of the fish and waft the smoke over the patient. For internal use the bones pulverised and mixed with water are taken.

NOTE.—This fish, by the Dutch called meerval, is said to be about a metre long, and though eaten with impunity by some, its flesh is evidently poisonous, and, according to reports, if taken will cause the flesh to fall from the bones. In accordance with a custom apparently universal among Dayaks, of leaving quarry for the women to bring home, the pâtin when caught is usually left at the landing float to be disposed of by the wife of the fisherman.

The Kiai Laman, a Kahayan, and a Mohammedan, who related the story, does not eat this fish, nor water turtle. Mr. B. Brouers, of Bandjermasin, whose mother was a Dayak noble from the Lower Kahayan, was instructed by her never to eat turtle. He, being a Dutchman, disregards this and nothing has ever happened, as he said, but he added that an acquaintance who did likewise lost the skin of his finger-tips.

22. THE STORY OF THE BIRD PUNAI

(From the Kahayans of Kuala Kapuas)

Long, long ago a man was catching punai with sticks to which glue had been applied. One was caught under the wing and fell to the ground. As he went to take it up it flew away a short distance. This happened several times, but at last he seized it, when suddenly it changed to a woman. He brought her to his house and said he wanted to make her his wife. "You may," she replied, "but you must never eat punai." This story happened in ancient times when many antohs were able to change into human beings.

The woman bore him many children. One day, when in a friend's house, people were eating punai, and he also ate some of it. His wife learned this and said to him: "I hear that you have eaten punai. You don't like me. I shall become a bird again." Since then her descendants have never eaten this bird, because they know that their great, great, great grandmother was a punai.

NOTE.—The punai is a light-green pigeon. Mata Punai (the eye of punai) is one of the most common decorative designs of many Dayak tribes.

23. RETRIBUTION

In the beginning there were mountain-tops and sea between them. Gradually the sea subsided and the land appeared. A man and a woman living on such a mountain-top had a son. One day a typhoon lifted him in the air and carried him off to Java, where he arrived in the house of a rich Javanese. This was long before the Hindu kingdom of Modjopahit. In this house he remained many years, and showed much intelligence and industry in his work, which was to cut wood, fish, look after the poultry, and clean the rooms. It was not necessary to give him orders, for he understood everything at a glance. By and by he became a trader, assisting his patron. Finally he married the rich man's only daughter, and after living happily a long time he remembered his parents, whom he had left in Borneo, desired to visit them, and asked his wife to accompany him.

They went in two ships, and, after sailing a month or more, came to a mountain, for there was no river then. When the ships arrived, prahus came out to ask their errand. "I am looking for my father and mother whom I left long ago," said the owner. They told him that his father was dead, but that his mother still lived, though very old.

The people went and told her that her son had come

to see her. She was very poor, for children there were none, and her husband was dead. Wearing old garments, and in a dilapidated prahu, she went out to the ships, where she made known that she wanted to see her anak (child). The sailors informed the captain that his mother was there, and he went to meet her, and behold! an old woman with white hair and soiled, torn clothing. "No!" he said, "she cannot be my mother, who was beautiful and strong." "I am truly your mother," she replied, but he refused to recognise her, and he took a pole (by which the prahus are poled) and drove her off.

She wept and said: "As I am your mother, and have borne you, I wish that your wife, your ships, and all your men may change into stone." The sky became dark, and thunder, lightning, and storm prevailed. The ships, the men, and the implements, everything, changed into stone, which to-day may be seen in these caves.

NOTE.—In the neighbourhood of Kandangan, a small town northward from Bandjermasin, are two mountains, one called gunong batu laki: the mountain of the stone man, the other gunong batu bini: the mountain of the stone wife. They contain large caves with stalactite formations which resemble human beings, ships, chairs, etc. The natives here visualise a drama enacted in the long gone-by, as related.

The Ex-Sultan of Pasir, a Malay then interned by the government in Bandjermasin, who was present when this story was told to me by a Mohammedan Kahayan, maintained that it is Dayak and said that it is also known in Pasir (on the east coast). Although the fact that the scene is laid in a region at present strongly Malay does not necessarily give a clew to the origin of the tale, still its contents are not such as to favour a Dayak source.

CONCLUSION

In closing this account of my investigations in Borneo it seems appropriate to comment briefly regarding the capabilities and future prospects of the tribes in Dutch Borneo comprised under the popular term Dayaks. We have seen that these natives are still inclined to the revolting habit of taking heads. In their dastardly attacks to accomplish this purpose, though moved by religious fanaticism, they show little courage. On the other hand they exhibit traits of character of which a civilised community might well be proud.

They are honest, trustworthy, and hospitable. In their kampongs a lonely stranger is safe from molestation and a white man travelling with them is far safer than with the Malays. They are able woodcraftsmen, and strikingly artistic, even their firewood being arranged in orderly fashion, pleasing to the eye. Should criticism arise regarding the unrestricted relations permitted in these tribes before marriage, owing to the fact that primitive conditions survive which are disapproved in civilised society, to their credit it must be admitted that conjugal relations are all that could be desired. A Dayak does not strike his wife, as Malays may do, and in business matters he takes her advice. During my travels I never heard of but one instance of infidelity. If such cases occur they are punished in some tribes with extreme severity.

In certain ways the Dayaks show more aptitude than

either Malays or Javanese. To illustrate—the young men of the latter races whom I employed as "boys" on various occasions, and the Javanese soldiers who accompanied me, were satisfactory on the whole, but when several work together, each one is afraid he will do more than his share. Neither of them can tie knots that are at once firm and readily undone, nor are they able to drive a nail properly, put in screws, or rope a box, although no doubt in time they could learn; but the Dayaks are uniformly handy at such work. A well-known characteristic of the "inlander," which he possesses in common with some classes in other races, is that if he receives his due, no more and no less, he accepts the payment without question, but if a gratuity is added he will invariably ask for more. The Dayaks are much easier to deal with in that regard and more businesslike.

Needless to state neither Javanese nor Malays are stupid. They learn quickly to do efficient routine work in office or shop, but when something new demands attention they are at a loss and appear awkward. Their intelligence, especially as regards the Javanese, is sometimes beyond the ordinary. Dr. J. C. Koningsberger, who at the time was director of the Botanic Garden at Buitenzorg, Java, told me that an "inlander" once applied to him for a position. He was able to read a little, but the doctor said: "I cannot employ you because you cannot write." A week later he returned and demonstrated that he had mastered the obstacle, having been taught by a friend in the evenings by lamplight. When clever, the Javanese are very clever.

The different tribes of Dayaks known to me are also quick of perception, intelligent, and, though varying in mental ability, some of them, as the Kahayans and the Duhoi, undoubtedly are capable of considerable attainment if given the opportunity. The Dutch missionary in Kasungan told me of a sixteen-year-old youth, a Duhoi, who was very ambitious to learn to read. Although he did not know the letters to start with, the missionary assured me that in two hours he was able to read short sentences.

It was always a pleasure to meet the unsophisticated Dayaks, and on leaving them I invariably felt a desire to return some day. What the future has in store for them is not difficult to predict, as the type is less persistent than the other with which it has to compete in this great island domain. Ultimately these natives, who on the whole are attractive, will be absorbed by the Malays; the latter, being naturally of roving disposition, travel much among the Dayaks, marry their women, and acquire their lands. The Malay trader takes his prahus incredibly far up the rivers. No place is so remote that beads, mirrors, cotton cloth, bright bandannas, sarongs for women, "made in Germany," etc., do not reach the aborigines, often giving them a Malay exterior, however primitive they may be in reality. The trader often remains away a year, marries a woman whom he brings back, and the children become Malays. In its assumed superiority the encroaching race is not unlike the common run of Mexicans who insidiously use the confiding Indians to advance their own interests. As Mohammedans, the aggressors feel contempt for the pork-eating natives, many of whom gradually give up this habit to attain what they consider a higher social status, at the same time adopting a new way of living, and eventually disappear.

In this manner a change is slowly but surely being wrought in the Dayaks, who regard the Malays as superior and are influenced accordingly; but the influence is not beneficial. Malays have been known to incite them to head-hunting, using them as tools for their own ends, and when entering upon one of their frequent revolutions always manage to enlist the support of Dayaks whom they have deceived by promises. The late comers have already occupied most of the main courses of the great rivers, and are constantly pressing the rightful owners back into the interior.

The Dutch officials, be it said to their credit, are helping the latter against the intruders, and at times the government has limited the activities of the Malays on some rivers. But it is difficult, and apparently impossible, to stop a process of absorption that began centuries ago. The ultimate extinction of the Dayak is inevitable because the Malay is not only stronger, but has the additional advantage of being more prolific.

SUPPLEMENTARY NOTES TO THE TRIBES IN DUTCH BORNEO VISITED BY THE AUTHOR

KAYANS

THE Kayans of Dutch Borneo are not numerous. Outside of Long Blu on the Mahakam they are found chiefly on the Kayan River in the large district of the northeast called Bulungan. They occupy the lower course, reaching not quite to Long Pangian, though having settlements there. Three subtribes are known to exist here, Oma-Gaai, Oma-Laran, and Oma-Hiban. The first named, also called Segai, live in Kaburau, Bruen, and Long Pangian. They appear somewhat different from the rest in language, and they abstain from rusa (deer) as food, while the others eat it. They file off ten teeth in the upper front jaw. At the headwaters of the Kayan River in Apo Kayan lives a subtribe, Oma-Lakan, said to number about 400; these do not file the front teeth. On page 87 is described a recent head-hunting raid by the Kenyahs on these Kayans.

KENYAHS

The Kenyahs are found only within the Bulungan district on the Kayan River. They are settled principally at the headwaters in Apo Kayan and at the sources of a northern tributary, the Bahau, in Podjungan. In these two regions it is estimated that they number altogether

425

about 25,000. Down the river they have a few kampongs below Long Pangian, in the same vicinity; west of it are a few more, as mentioned in the description of my journey. On attempting to ascend the river further one would soon reach a vast extent of country entirely uninhabited except around the headwaters. The Bahau, too, is inhabited only at its source, and both rivers pass through wild, picturesque regions.

On that portion of the Kayan called Brem-Brem the river presents a formidable array of kihams which defeated the government's attempt to establish communication between Apo Kayan and the debouchure of the river. This was desirable for the sake of provisioning the garrison. An officer of the Dutch army in Borneo told me that from military reports and the testimony of Kenyahs he estimated that the Brem-Brem is a continuous stretch of kihams for thirty kilometres. The Kenyahs had told him that they walked two days and he thought that for four kilometres the river ran underground. These difficult conditions compel the Kenyahs to take another route in their travels to Tandjong Selor, marching over the watershed to the Bahau River, where they make new prahus and then continue the journey.

I give a list of subtribes with reserve:

Oma-Bakkah, Oma-Lisan, Oma-Kulit, Oma-Lim, Oma-Puah, Oma-Yalan, Oma-Tokkung, Oma-Bakkung, Oma-Bam, Oma-Lung, Oma-Badang, Lepo-Tepó, Lepo-Táo, Lepo-Maot, Lepo-Ké Anda Páh, Lepo-Ké Ang Lung, Lepo-Ké Oma-Lasang. Most of the Lepo are on the Bahau. My informant, who had travelled in the interior, said there was little difference in the languages of these subtribes.

The Kenyahs, a few Kayans, and the Katingans mutilate the membrum virile by transpiercing the glans and the urethra, and a piece of brass wire is inserted. A Kenyah tribe (Oma-Badang) in Podjungan, makes two perforations so directed that the wires are crossed.

The kapala of the Penihing kampong Long Kai, on the Mahakam, told me that Kayan and Kenyah are the same people. He probably knew the Kayans only by personal experience, but his opinion is curious in view of the fact that the two tribes have been bracketed by Dr. A. C. Haddon and Dr. J. H. F. Kohlbrugge.

MURUNGS

(Notes from kampong Tumbang Marowei, on the Laong, a tributary to the Barito River, in Central Borneo)

At the time of childbirth two to four women and one blian attend the prospective mother, who assumes a recumbent position with the upper portion of the body slightly raised. The blian blows upon a cupful of water which the woman drinks in order to make delivery easy. The umbilical cord is cut with a knife or a sharp piece of ironwood, and the afterbirth is buried. Death in labor is not unknown, and twins are born occasionally. The mother is confined for a week, and she is forbidden to eat pork, eggs, new rice, cocoanut oil, or any acid substance. She may partake of ordinary rice, lombok (red pepper), as well as sugar, and all kinds of fruit except bananas. She bathes three times a day, as is her usual custom. In one week, as soon as the navel is healed, two or three fowls are killed, or a pig, and a small feast is held at which rice brandy is served. The child is suckled for one year.

No name is given the infant until it can eat rice, which is about five months after birth. At the age of six years, or when it begins to take part in the work of the paddi fields, fishing, etc., the name is changed. In both cases the father gives the name. The kapala, my informant, changed his name a third time about ten years previously, when he entered the service of the government. Names are altered for the purpose of misleading evil spirits.

Children were few here, one reason being that abortion is a common practice, as is instanced in the case of the kapala's wife who prided herself on her success in this regard on ten occasions. Massage as well as abortifacient herbs are employed for the purpose. The root of a plant in general use is soaked in water before administering. I was also shown a vine which was about two centimetres in diameter and was told that if a portion of this was cut off and the end inserted into a pint bottle the vine would yield sufficient juice to fill it in a night. In case children are not wanted both husband and wife drink of this liquid after the morning meal, and both abstain from water for the remainder of the day. It is believed that afterward it would be possible for the man to have offspring only by marrying a new wife. There are also several specifics to prevent conception, but none for producing fertility. The kapala gave as reasons for this practice scarcity of food and woman's fear of dying. Both seem incongruous to fact and primitive ideas, and perhaps his view would better be accepted only as an indication of his ignorance in the matter. The young people are taught to dance by the blian before they are married, and take lessons for a year or two.

The Murung blian possesses three small wooden statues of human beings which he employs in recovering brua (souls) and bringing them back to persons who are ill, thus making them well. These images are called jurong, two being males, the other female, and carrying a child on its back. While performing his rites over either sex the blian holds the female jurong in his right hand, the other two being inserted under his girdle, one in front, the other at the back, to protect him against his enemies. In the case of a child being ill its brua is brought back by means of the infant carved on the back of the effigy. Undoubtedly the images are similar in character to the kapatongs I have described as occupying an important place in the lives of the Duhoi (Ot-Danum), the Katingan, and other tribes of Southwestern Borneo.

PENYAHBONGS

(Notes from the Upper Busang River, Central Borneo)

The Dutch officials give this tribe the name of Punan-Penyahbongs; the Malays call them Punans, seldom Penyahbongs. The Saputans, a neighbouring tribe, told me that the Penyahbongs and the Punans make themselves mutually understood. Whether they really are Punans or have been called so because of their recent nomadic habits is difficult to determine. However, since they declare themselves to be Punans, in view of all related circumstances it is safe to conclude that they are allied to that great nomadic tribe.

According to the Penihing chief in Long Kai the name Penyahbong was applied formerly not only to the people, but also to the mountain range in which they were living, the Müller mountains, around the headwaters of the Kapuas River in the Western Division. The western sides of the Müller mountains seem to have been their headquarters, and most of them still live west of the mountains. To one of the tributaries of this river the tribe owes the name by which they are known among Punans, Saputans, and Bukats, who call the Penyahbongs simply Kreho.

They are not numerous and so far as my information goes they are limited to a few hundred. Gompul, the most reliable of my Malays in that region, and one of the first to arrive in those parts, told me that his mother had been captured by the Penyahbongs and kept by them for thirty-five years, until her death. According to his estimate there were over two hundred of them in the Müller mountains, and they had killed many Malays, taking their heads. Three chiefs were famous for being very tall.

Fishing with tuba is known to them, also to the nomadic Punans and Bukats, Saputans, and Penihings. The Penyahbongs believe they were placed in this world by an antoh. Omens are taken from nine birds and from dreams. When a house is finished there are two or three hours' dancing in the night by men and women, one man playing the sapi (native guitar).

The child is born outside of the house. One or two women stand by to take it, wrapped in cloth, into the dwelling, where for three days it remains unbathed. Although death at childbirth is known to occur, usually within fifteen minutes the mother rises and repairs to the house. The umbilical cord is cut with a sharp bamboo and the afterbirth is not taken care of, dogs generally being permitted to eat it. When the child can walk the father and mother give it a name. No abortion is practised, there are no puberty ceremonies, and sexual intercourse is not practised during menstruation.

SAPUTANS
(Notes from the Kasao River, a tributary to the Upper Mahakam)

The name Saputan is derived from the word sahput, sumpitan (the blow-pipe), and probably means, "those who have sumpitan." In the upper part of the Kasao River is a big back current called Saputan and the people who originally lived at the headwaters have the same name as the current. At first they were roaming in the mountains, though not conflicting with the Penyahbongs, and later settled in four kampongs which, beginning with the uppermost, at the time of my visit were: 1. Pomosing (mouse) at a tributary of the same name. 2. Data Láong (land of durian). 3. Ong Sangi (ong = river). 4. Nomorunge (a common, small, black and white bird) on a tributary of the same name; with hardly a hundred full-grown persons, this is the largest. Formerly the office of the chief, tjúpi, was hereditary. When he became old he was succeeded by his son.

The woman bears her child in the house, surrounded by women, her husband, and another man. She assumes a lying position and is helped by being frequently lifted up, and by stroking. The abdomen is rubbed with a certain medicinal herb, first having been heated over the fire, to facilitate the expulsion of the afterbirth, which later is hung in a tree. Having tied a vine round the umbilical cord near the abdomen they cut the cord with a sharp piece of bamboo. The assisting women wash the baby as well as the mother.

For two days after childbirth she does no work, and for some time she must not eat the fat of pig or fish. In case of twins being born, they are welcome if the sex is the same, but if one is male and the other female, one is given away, the father exercising his preference. Two months after birth a name is given by the father. Should the mother die, no other woman willingly suckles the child unless the father has a daughter who can do it. However, by paying from one to three gongs a woman may be induced to undertake the duty.

ORANG BAHAU
(On the Mahakam River)

Bahau is the name of a river in Apo Kayan, where the tribes of the Mahakam River lived before they migrated to their present habitations, a hundred and fifty to two hundred years ago. The Penihings, Kayans, Oma-Sulings, and Long-Glats speak of themselves as Orang Bahau, as also do the Saputans, though probably they did not originally come from Apo Kayan. According to these Dayaks the designation as used by the Malays signifies people who wear only chavat (loin cloth), and the Punans and Ibans are said to be included under the same term.

PUNANS AND BUKATS

(Notes from kampong Long Kai on the Mahakam River)

The formidable king cobra (*naia bungarus*) is feared by the Punans, who have no remedy for the bite of this or any other venomous snake. The Bukats are said to know a cure which they share with the Penihings; the bark is scraped from a certain tree and the juice is applied to the wound. Death from lightning is unknown to any of these three tribes.

The Punans apparently do not attribute disease to the adverse influence of an antoh, although their remedy is the same, consisting of singing in the night and removing small stones from the abdomen or other parts that may be affected.

The Bukats whom I met were beautifully tatued. The kapala whom I saw at Long Kai had the mark of a ripe durian on each shoulder in front and an immature one above each nipple. On the lower part of the upper arm was a tatu of an edible root, in Penihing called rayong. Over the back of his right hand, toward the knuckles, he had a zigzag mark representing the excrescences of the durian fruit. In regard to the presence of spirits, number of souls, blians, disease, and its cure, restrictions for pregnant women, the child's cradle—the ideas of the Bukats are identical with those of the Penihings, and possibly are derived from them.

PENIHINGS

(Notes from the Mahakam River)

The Penihings get their supply of ipoh, the poison for the sumpitan darts, from Punans who live at the sources of the rivers of the Western Division. According to native report the trees which furnish the juice do not grow along the Mahakam and the nearest country where they are found is to the south of Tamaloë. As is the case with the Punans and Bukats, cutting the teeth is optional.

Restrictions imposed during pregnancy do not differ from those of other tribes described. At childbirth no man is permitted to be present. For three days the mother eats boiled rice, red pepper, and barks of certain trees, and she may work on the third day. Twins are known to occur. As soon as the navel is healed a name is given to the child. Both Penihing and Saputan, if asked, are allowed to give their own names. Marriages are contracted while the woman is still a child. There are no marriage ceremonies and divorces are easily obtained. If a married woman is at fault with another man the two must pay the injured husband one gong, as well as one gong for each child. In case the husband is at fault, the same payment is exacted by the injured wife.

The Penihings have a game called ot-tjin which I also observed in other Bornean tribes, and which to some extent is practised by the Malays. This game, generally known among scientific men by the name mancala, is of the widest distribution. Every country that the Arabs have touched has it, and it is found practically in every African tribe. It is very common in the coffee houses of Jerusalem and Damascus. A comprehensive account of the game mancala is given by Mr. Stewart Culin, the eminent authority on games, in the Report of the U. S. National Museum for 1894, pages 595–607.

With the Penihings the complete name is aw-li on-nam ot-tjin, meaning: play on-nam fish. An essential of the game is an oblong block of heavy wood which on its upper surface is provided with two rows of shallow holes, ten in each row, also a larger one at each end. The implement is called tu-tung ot-tjin, as is also both of the large single holes at the ends. There are two players who sit opposite each other, each controlling ten holes. The stake may be ten or twenty wristlets, or perhaps a fowl, or the black rings that are tied about the upper part of the calf of the leg, but not money, because usually there is none about. The game is played in the evenings.

Two, three, four, or five stones of a small fruit may be put in each hole; I noticed they generally had three; pebbles may be used instead. Let us suppose two have been placed in each hole; the first player takes up two from any hole on his side. He then deposits one in the hole next following. Thus we have three in each of these two holes. He takes all three from the last hole and deposits one in each of the next three holes; from the last hole he again takes all three, depositing one in each of the next three holes. His endeavour is to get two stones in a hole and thus make a "fish." He proceeds until he reaches an empty hole, when a situation has arisen which is called gok—that is to say, he must stop, leaving his stone there.

His adversary now begins on his side wherever he likes, proceeding in the same way, from right to left,

THE GAME MANCALA AS USED BY THE PENIHINGS.

until he reaches an empty hole, which makes him gok, and he has to stop.

To bring together two stones in one hole makes a "fish," but if three stones were originally placed in each hole, then three make a "fish"; if four were originally placed, then four make a "fish," etc., up to five. The player deposits the "fish" he gains to the right in the single hole at the end.

The two men proceed alternately in this manner, trying to make "fish" (ára ot-tjin). The player is stopped in his quest by an empty hole; there he deposits his last stone and his adversary begins. During the process of taking up and laying down the stones no hole is omitted; in some of them the stones will accumulate. On the occasion of the game described I saw two with eight in them.

When one of the players has no stones left in his holes he has lost. If stones are left on either side, but not enough to proceed, then there is an impasse, and the game must be played over again.

OMA–SULINGS

(On the Mahakam River)

To marry the daughter of a noble the man must pay her father twenty to thirty gongs (each costing twenty to forty florins). The price of the daughter of a pangawa is from one to three gongs, and to obtain a wife from the family of a pangin costs a parang, a knife, or some beads. Women assist at childbirth, which takes place within the room, near the door, but generally no blian is present.

When a girl has her first menstruation a hen or a pig is killed, and in the evening the blood thus obtained is applied to the inside of a folded leaf which the blian wafts down her arms—"throwing away illness," the meat of the sacrifice being eaten as usual. The same treatment is bestowed upon any one who desires good health.

As many infants die, it is the custom to wait eight or ten days after birth before naming a child, when a similar sacrifice is made, and a leaf prepared in like manner is passed down the arms of the infant by the blian. In selecting a name he resorts to an omen, cutting two pieces of a banana leaf into the shape of smaller leaves. According to the way these fall to the ground the matter is decided. If after two trials the same result is obtained the proposed name is considered appropriate. Also on the occasion of marriage, a similar sacrifice and the same curative practice are used.

When couples tire of each other they do not quarrel. The husband seeks another wife and she another husband, the children remaining with the mother. The sacred numbers of the Oma-Sulings are four, eight, and sixteen. Contact with a woman's garment is believed to make a man weak, therefore is avoided.

The interpretation of designs in basketwork, etc., is identical with the Oma-Sulings and the Penihings, though the women of the last-named tribe are better informed on the subject.

The antoh usually recognised by the name nagah, is called āso (dog) lidjau by the Oma-Sulings and Long-Glats, while among the Penihings and Punans it is known as tjingiru, but nagah is the name used also in Southern Borneo, where I frequently noticed it in designs. On the Mahakam few are the Oma-Suling and Long-Glat houses which are not decorated with an artistic representation of this antoh. Among the Penihings in Long Tjehan I never saw a sword hilt carved with any other motif. On the knife-handle it is also very popular.

There are three modes of disposing of the dead: by burying in the ground a metre deep; by depositing the coffin in a cave, or by making a house, called bila, inside of which the coffin is placed. A raja is disposed of according to either the second or third method, but the ordinary people of the kampong are placed in the ground.

LONG–GLATS

(Notes from Long Tujo, Mahakam River)

Before they emigrated from Apo Kayan the name of the Long-Glats was Hu-van-ke-raw. Attached to Long Tujo is a small kampong occupied by the Oma-Tapi, who speak a different language, and almost opposite, scarcely a kilometre down the river, is another inhabited by the Oma-Lokvi, who speak a dialect other than Long-Glat. Not far west of here is a kampong, Nahamerang, where the Bato-Pola live, said to be Kayan. The Long-Glats appear to be powerful, but their measurements are very irregular. They seem darker in colour than the other Bahau people, most of them showing twenty-six on the von Luschan colour scale.

Pregnant women and their husbands are subject to restrictions similar to those already described in regard to other tribes. In addition may be mentioned that they must not eat two bananas that have grown together, nor sugar-cane which the wind has blown to the ground, nor rice if it has boiled over the kettle, nor fish which in being caught has fallen to the ground or in the boat. The afterbirth drops through the floor and is eaten by dogs or pigs. The still-born child is wrapped in a mat and placed in a hollow tree. The mother may work in five days. Two to four weeks elapse before the child is named by the blian and this ceremony is accompanied by the sacrifice of a pig. In cases of divorce the children may follow either parent according to agreement.

The coffin is a log hollowed out, and provided with

a cover. At one end is carved the head of Panli, an antoh, and at the other his tail. Many vestments are put on the corpse, and for a man a parang is placed by his side within the coffin. The house is then made and the coffin placed inside.

DUHOI (Ot-Danums)

(Notes from the Samba River, Southwestern Borneo)

The new-born child is washed with water of that which is brought to the mother, and the afterbirth is thrown into the river. Most of the women, after bearing a child in the morning, walk about in the afternoon, though some have to wait a few days. Their food for some time is rice and fish, abstaining from salt, lombok (red pepper), fat, acid, and bitter food, also meat.

Seven days after birth the child is taken to the river to be bathed. On its return blood from a fowl or, if people are well to do, from a pig that has been sacrificed, is smeared on its forehead and chest, and a name is given. The presence of the blian not being required, the parents give the name, which is taken from a plant, tree, flower, animal, or fish. A wristlet is placed around each wrist and the name is not changed later in life. There are no puberty nor menstruation ceremonies. No sexual intercourse is permissible while a woman is pregnant, nor during menstruation, nor during the first three months after childbirth. Cousins may marry.

Evidence of polyandry is found among the Duhoi. Eight years previous to my visit on the river Braui lived for six years a woman blian about thirty years old, who had three young husbands. She practised her profession and the husbands gathered rattan and rubber. She was known to have had thirty-three husbands, keeping a man a couple of weeks, or as many months, then taking others. She had no children.

A design representing the flying prahu, described on page 336, is also occasionally seen in Kahayan mats, the idea being that it may be of assistance to some beneficent antoh. In this connection it is of interest to note how the Kahayans use the flying prahu as a feature of the great tiwah festival. Drawings of the craft are made in colours on boards which are placed in the house of ceremonies, and are intended to serve as a conveyance for the liao. Such drawings are also presented to the good antoh, Sangiang, as a reward for his assistance in making the feast successful, thus enabling him to fly home.

UPPER AND LOWER KATINGANS
(Southwestern Borneo)

Of the Dayaks living about the headwaters of the Katingan River Controleur Michielsen, in his report quoted before, says: "I cannot omit here to mention that the Dayaks of these regions in language and habits show the closest agreement with the Alfurs in Central Celebes, whom I visited in 1869, and that most of the words of the Alfur language (which I at once understood because it resembles the low Java language) also here in the Dayak language were observed by me. This circumstance affords convincing testimony in favour of the early existence of a Polynesian language stock and for a common origin of the oldest inhabitants of the archipelago."

There appears to be much similarity in regulations regarding marriage, birth, death, and other adats as observed by the Katingans, Duhoi, and Mehalats. The latter, who live on the Senamang, a tributary to the Katingan River near its headwater, may be a Duhoi subtribe, but very little is known about them; the custom of drinking tuak from human skulls is credited to them, and they are looked upon with contempt by the Katingans for eating dogs.

With the Katingans it is the custom for the blian to deposit in a cup containing uncooked rice the objects withdrawn from a patient. Having danced and spoken to the cereal he throws it away and with it the articles, the rice advising the antoh that the small stones, or whatever was eliminated, which he placed in the patient, are now returned to him.

These Katingans begin their year in June and July, when they cut the jungle in order to make ladangs, months being designated by numbers. At the beginning of the year all the families sacrifice fowls, eat the meat, and give the blood to antoh in accordance with their custom. After the harvest there is a similar function at which the same kind of dancing is performed as at the tiwah feast. On both occasions a game is engaged in which also is found among the Bahau and other tribes, wherein a woman jumps dexterously between heavy pestles that, held horizontally, are lifted up and brought down in rapid succession. Three months later—at the end of the year—another festival occurs.

The Katingan calendar may be rendered thus:

1. Cutting the jungle, June and July....... during 2 months
2. Drying the trees and burning them...... " 1 month
3. Planting paddi....................... " 2 months
4. New paddi........................... in 3 months
5. Harvesting........................... during 1 or 2 months
6. Waiting............................. " 3 months

In order to ascertain the auspicious date for planting paddi these Dayaks employ an astronomical device founded on the obvious fact that in their country there comes a period when a rod placed in an upright position casts no shadow. That is the time for planting. In addition to this method of determination they consult a constellation of three stars which "rise" in the east and "set" in the west during half a year, and are invisible during the following six months. When the three stars appear perpendicularly above the rod in the early morning, before sunrise, then the time to plant is at hand; when they are in the zenith in the late afternoon before sunset, the season for making ladang has come.

For these observations, however, a single rod is not used, but an arrangement of rods called togallan, seven in number, which are planted in the ground, the middle one upright, the rest diverging on either side like a fan. Beginning on the left side, six months are indicated, but the togallan does not remain standing more than three; in fact as soon as the planting is finished it is removed. Although the most propitious time is when the sun is at zenith, it is also considered favourable for half the distance from the middle rod toward 3 and toward 5. If paddi is planted in the second month the crop will be injured; if in the fifth month, the plant will be damaged.

Formerly heavy spears made of ironwood were employed not only as weapons, but for agricultural purposes

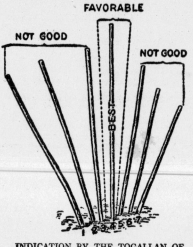

INDICATION BY THE TOGALLAN OF
THE FAVORABLE TIME FOR
PLANTING RICE.

as well, both when making the holes into which the seed grains are dropped and as material in erecting the astronomical device. Each of the seven rods is called tondang, as is the pointed stick with which at present the ground is prepared for planting paddi.

MISCELLANEOUS

With the Kenyahs and many other tribes it is the custom to give boiled rice that has stood overnight to

KENYAH WOMEN HUSKING RICE. LONG PELABAN,
KAYAN RIVER

KATINGAN TAKING AN ASTRONOMICAL OBSERVATION.
KASUNGAN

A TAILLESS DOG, SISTER OF THE
MOTHER OF THE STUMP-TAILED
ONES. BANDJERMASIN

THE SHORT-TAILED DOMESTIC CAT
OF BORNEO

A BREED OF STUMP-TAILED DOGS. BANDJERMASIN

the dogs, pigs, and hens; it is not considered fit for human food.

Regarding the number of souls: The Murung says that each person has seven souls, called brua, six being distributed as follows: one at the top of the head, one in each eye and knee, and one in the navel. The Duhoi (Ot-Danum) has also seven brua, one at the top of the head and one in each eye, knee, and wrist.

Other tribes speak of three souls. The Kenyahs, according to Dr. J. M. Elshout, have only one brua, located at times in the head, at times in the heart; and the tiger-cat and the orang-utan have stronger brua than man. The Katingans likewise recognise but one, called liao in life, and after death. They also give the same name to the soul of an animal, but the more common usage in the tribes is to call the ghost liao, by the Malays named njava.

In regard to the practice of incision, which is used in Southwest Borneo, page 379, I am able to furnish some details gathered in Sampit from three Dayaks who had been operated upon. A cut is made in the præputium lengthwise with a knife (further east a sharpened bamboo is used), a piece of ironwood being used as a support, and the operation which in Katingan is called habálak is performed by the father of the father's brother when the boy is coming of age. Before the event he must go into the river up to his navel seven days in succession, morning, midday, and evening, and stand in the water for an hour. All boys must undergo the operation, which is not sanguinary, the leaves of a tree called mentawa being applied to the wound. They could give no reason why they follow this practice any more than the ordinary Dayak can explain the purpose of tatuing.

With the Kayans, and, indeed, all the tribes I met in Dutch Borneo, it is the custom to urinate in a sitting position.

To the observer it is strikingly evident that the mammæ of both Dayak and Malay women retain firmness and shape much longer than is the case with white women.

A SHORT GLOSSARY

adat, precept, regulation, religious observance.

antoh, spirit, good or evil.

atap, a shelter, consisting of a mat resting on upright saplings, often erected in the boats on long journeys.

babi, pig.

badak, rhinoceros.

balei, a general name for a house of worship.

barang, goods, things, belongings.

blanga, large, valuable jar, usually of Chinese manufacture.

blian, priest-doctor.

bom, custom-house.

brua, soul.

chavat, loin-cloth.

company (the), the government.

cranyang, basket.

damar, resin.

gutshi, large jar.

inlander, native.

ipoh, poison for the dart of the blowpipe, also the tree from which it is secured (the upas tree).

kali, river.

kampong, native village.

kapala, chief (=pumbakal).

kidyang, a small kind of deer.

kiham, rapids.

kuala, mouth of a river.

ladang, paddi field.

laki, man, male.

lombok, red pepper.

mandau, Dayak short sword (=parang).

mandur, overseer.

nagah, fabulous animal, the apparition of a spirit.

onder, native subdistrict chief.

orang, man.

paddi, rice.

parang, Dayak short sword (=mandau).

pasang-grahan, public lodging-house.

pisau, small knife.

plandok, mouse-deer (*tragulus*).

prahu, native boat.

pumbakal, chief (=kapala).

raja, a native chief, or noble.

raja besar, big raja.
ringit, the Dutch coin of f. 2.50.
rupia, florin, guilder.
rusa, deer.

sambir, mat made from palm leaves.
sarong, a cloth wound around the loins.
sayur, vegetable stew.
sumpitan, blowpipe.

takut, timid.
ticcar, mat made from rattan.

tin, five-gallon tin can.
tingang, great hornbill.
tingeling, scaly ant-eater.
tuak, native rice brandy.
tuan, master, lord.
tuan besar, great master or lord.
tuba, root used for poisoning the water for fishing purposes.

utan, jungle, woods.

wah-wah, gibbon, a long-armed monkey.
wang, coin, money.

INDEX